How to Pick
QUALITY
SHARES

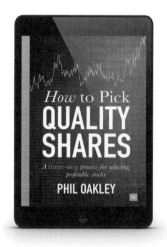

How to Pick
QUALITY
SHARES

A three-step *process for selecting
profitable stocks*

PHIL OAKLEY

Hh Harriman House

HARRIMAN HOUSE LTD
18 College Street
Petersfield
Hampshire
GU31 4AD
GREAT BRITAIN
Tel: +44 (0)1730 233870

Email: enquiries@harriman-house.com
Website: www.harriman-house.com

First published in Great Britain in 2017.

Print ISBN: 978-0-85719-534-0
eBook ISBN: 978-0-85719-607-1

British Library Cataloguing in Publication Data

A CIP catalogue record for this book can be obtained from the British Library.

CONTENTS

ABOUT THE AUTHOR

Phil Oakley is an investment analyst and private investor. He works for Ionic Information, the makers of the market-leading ShareScope and SharePad software for private investors.

Phil spent 13 years as a professional investment analyst, with ten years working for fund managers and stockbrokers in the City. He left the City in 2009 and began writing educational articles for private investors. He was senior investment writer for *MoneyWeek* for three years before starting his current role.

He holds the Chartered Institute of Securities & Investment Diploma and the Certificate in Private Client Investment Advice & Management.

Phil lives in Essex with his wife and two children. You can read more of his writing at **www.sharescope.co.uk/philoakley.**

PREFACE

What this book covers

THIS BOOK IS about how investors can assess companies and find good share investments by following a three-step strategy to analyse company financial information. The strategy boils down to finding quality companies, avoiding dangerous or risky companies, and not paying too much for companies' shares.

For the first step, I show you how to identify companies that are capable of earning you a high rate of interest on your investment. These are the kind of companies that can prove to be profitable investments over the long term. You may not be accustomed to thinking of an investment return as a rate of interest, but I will show you that this can help you understand companies and their shares better, and make you a better investor.

Next, good investing is just as much about risk as it is about returns. By avoiding risky companies, you stand a better chance of being a successful investor. I show you how to spot the warning signs of companies that would make bad investments.

Third, no matter how good a company is, its shares are never a good buy at *any* price. I show how to value a company's shares and determine what is a reasonable price to pay. I also show that whilst you should always try to buy your shares as cheaply as possible, it is important to realise that sometimes you have to pay more for quality companies.

Following these three steps, you are trying to answer three important questions about a company:

1. Is it a quality business?

2. Is it a safe business?

3. Are its shares cheap enough – are they good value?

I use real companies as examples throughout the book. In particular, I focus on Domino's Pizza. This is because it is a high-quality company that most people should find easy to understand, whilst allowing me to illustrate many of the things you need to look for in order to follow the three-step strategy.

The focus in the book is on UK companies, but readers can use the techniques to analyse companies anywhere in the world.

To make use of the process described in the book, you will need to have access to company accounts and financial statements. These are publicly available for all stock market-listed companies. You can find this information in the investor section on company websites, or in commercial stock market software packages.

Note that the approach in the book is very much one of quantitative analysis – looking at company financial information. Qualitative analysis – such as looking at the character and capability of company management – is not part of the process described here.

Also note that this book is to be used to appraise investments in non-financial companies. The tools of analysis found in this book are not suitable for looking at banks or insurance companies, which require a different approach.

Who this book is for

This is not a book aimed at complete beginners. It is aimed at the more experienced investor who manages his or her own portfolio of individual shares.

Readers should have some knowledge about company accounts. You should have a general understanding of an income statement, balance sheet and cash flow statement. Terms like assets, liabilities, cash inflow and cash outflow should be familiar to you. I explain how to get the most from these valuable bits of information.

The mere thought of numbers and maths can frighten some people and make them think that investing is too difficult. I will show you that **this is not the case**. It is not necessary to have a high IQ or to have a degree to become a good investor and as long as you understand basic GCSE-level arithmetic you will be fine.

This book is aimed at long-term investors rather than short-term traders. It is not about getting rich quickly, but about finding companies to invest in over a long period of time – perhaps for the rest of your life.

To get the most from this strategy you should be prepared to spend some time researching companies when you are building your portfolio. Once your portfolio is set up, looking after it should not take up much of your time.

Investors do not need to own lots of shares. A portfolio of 10 to 15 shares spread across different industries is sufficient to get good, diversified investment results. My view is that an individual investment of £3000 to £5000 in each company is an acceptable minimum, which means that you will need a minimum of £30,000 at the outset before you begin investing.

More than anything, this is a book for people who are independent thinkers and are confident in trusting their own judgement whilst ignoring the huge amount of noise and chatter that goes on in the investing world.

How this book is structured

The structure of this book is based around the three-step process for finding good companies, avoiding dangerous companies and buying shares at a reasonable price. The three main parts of the book mirror these three steps.

Part 1: How To Find Quality Companies

Part 1 is all about the hallmarks of quality companies and how you can spot these in a company's accounts.

I show how to work out a company's *interest rate* on the money it invests, which measure of profit to focus on, and why you should make a company's cash flow one of the main focuses of your attention.

Part 2: How To Avoid Dangerous Companies

Successful investing is just as much about avoiding bad companies as it is picking good ones. Just as you wouldn't buy a house without checking if it is structurally sound, you shouldn't invest in a share without seeing if it has any nasty risks that could cost you money.

In Part 2, I look in detail at the issue of debt, when it can be dangerous and how it can fool investors. I then discuss the often-overlooked issues of hidden debts and pension fund black holes.

Part 3: How To Value A Company's Shares

Part 3 begins with a basic lesson on how shares are valued. I then go on to show you why some of the most common shortcuts used to value shares are not very useful and indicate what you should be doing instead.

I then look at how to calculate a company's cash profits so that you can value a company's shares properly. Once this has been done you will then be able to work out the cash interest rate a share will earn you, which enables you to compare it with the interest rate you earn on other investments. You can then work out the maximum price you should pay for it.

Finally, I look at the importance of growth to the value of shares. You will learn to work out the stock market's expectation of future profit growth from a company's share price and also see how you can lose a lot of money when profits stop growing.

Appendices

In the Appendices I include the results of a 2016 experiment into a lease-adjusted version of Joel Greenblatt's Magic Formula, and also a table showing results for investment quality measures (as defined in Part 1) for companies from the FTSE 100. Finally, I provide examples of 15 high-quality companies that would have been very strong performing investments over the ten years since 2007.

INTRODUCTION

MY INVESTING CAREER began in May 1997, working for a relatively small wealth management firm in Liverpool as an analyst. My job was to research the shares of many different companies and advise the company's portfolio managers who looked after customers' money.

City brokers didn't talk to us because we weren't big enough to pay them for their research. At first, I thought that put us at a big disadvantage. However, a few years later I realised the opposite was in fact true. Being able to think independently is the best way to invest successfully.

I enjoyed my job in Liverpool but the problem was that it didn't pay well and didn't offer much in terms of career progression. So after a couple of years I accepted a higher-paying role as an analyst working for a stockbroking firm as a transport analyst. This was my introduction to the big world of the City.

Being an analyst in the City was an extremely privileged position. Not only did I get to work with some great people with great minds, but I got to meet people who ran companies that were worth millions – sometimes billions – of pounds, and which provided fantastic products and services. It was a superb education into how businesses work.

I spent ten years in the City before leaving to try something new. There were many reasons for this, including the long hours and the lack of time with my young family. I had also become disillusioned with how the City works.

It was nothing to do with some of the well-publicised scandals of recent years. In fact, I can truthfully say that the people I worked with were some of the most honest, decent and nicest people you could wish to meet. No, it was because of the way a lot of the City looked after its customers' money.

At root, the problem is that the way professional fund managers are remunerated means they are encouraged to act in a similar way. The result is that many professionally-managed portfolios are very similar to each other and they fail to offer investors a genuinely differentiated product. It doesn't need to be this way and there are some brilliant fund managers out there, but this is how many large funds operate in the current situation. And so I left the City and went in a new direction.

My approach to investing

When investing for my own personal portfolios, I have not always followed the three-step process explained in this book. It took years of learning and lots of mistakes before I found that this process worked for me.

When I first started running my own share portfolios, I tried to practise what many people call value investing. My approach involved buying shares in beaten-up companies whose share prices had become depressed and looked cheap.

Occasionally, some investments would pay off, but more often than not they didn't. What I had failed to realise was that shares can be cheap for a reason – if they are shares of bad or mediocre companies. It was like buying a cheap bottle of wine and expecting it to taste great – this isn't always going to work out for the best.

I needed to find a way of investing which didn't involve chasing poor companies. The good news is that there is one. It is very simple and can be very effective, so much so that you do not need to be a full-time investor to benefit from it. You just need to be disciplined and patient.

Good investing is about investing in great companies by buying their shares at reasonable prices and holding on to them for a long time. Great companies generate high levels of profits or cash flows on the money they invest, which I refer to as the company having a high interest rate. Your job as an investor is to buy the shares of these companies when their share prices offer you an acceptable return on your investment. Combining quality companies and a reasonable purchase price, and adding in the factor of time, puts you well on the way to a successful investing career.

I have no doubt that the diligent investor can manage their own portfolio of shares as well as – if not better than – many highly-paid fund managers. I say this because successful investing is not about being clever or having access to huge amounts of information.

In fact, too much information can be bad for you. It can make you think that you know more than you really do and this can lead you to make mistakes as a result of overconfidence. Professional analysts and fund managers may work long hours, but you do not need to know everything about a company to be a successful investor.

If you have a company's latest annual report and its current share price you have all the information you need to invest profitably. From this information, you can work out whether a company is good or bad, whether it is safe or dangerous, and whether its shares are cheap or expensive.

The methods of analysis that I explain in this book are more advanced than in many investing books and they may seem complicated at first, but they are not. As you read, you may think to yourself that this seems like an involved process to go through, and why not just leverage off of the work of professional analysts, who have done all of these calculations already, by reading their reports? Or why not just buy a fund managed by a professional manager, whose team of analysts will have done all of this number crunching already?

The answer is that *many analysts do not follow the steps in this book* and, even if they do, they can make mistakes, interpret the data incorrectly, or fail to be thorough enough. That is where the investor – armed with annual reports and a thorough approach – can gain an advantage. When you hear about successful investors, the kind of thorough analysis they are doing is the kind of analysis I describe in this book. Doing this kind of in-depth analysis for companies you are considering as investments will empower you with knowledge and understanding about a company which less diligent investors will not be aware of.

I hope that by following the three-step process in this book you will develop the confidence and ability to analyse companies and find rewarding investments.

We begin with Part 1, which looks at the first step: how to find quality companies.

PART 1

HOW TO FIND QUALITY COMPANIES

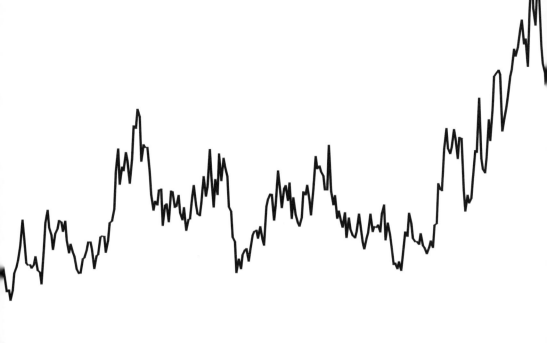

PART 1 – HOW TO FIND QUALITY COMPANIES

IF YOU ARE going to be a confident, self-reliant investor then you will be spending time looking at a company's finances. The numbers in a company's accounts are extremely valuable information. They can help you identify great investment opportunities and keep you away from bad ones.

Despite the fact that these numbers are freely available to every investor, many fail to get the most out of them. A large number of investors – even professional ones – are quite lazy.

This is where the diligent investor can gain an advantage. By spending just a little bit of time crunching a few numbers you can quickly build up a picture of how good a company is. This is the focus of Part 1. The good news is that this only requires a bit of basic arithmetic in most cases.

Chapter 1 is all about profits. It begins by explaining all the different profit numbers that a company reports before telling you which profit number you should use to find the best companies.

Chapter 2 is the most important in the book. It is about getting you to think about shares like savings accounts. You do this by calculating a company's interest rate – what rate of return it is getting on the money it invests. You will be introduced to a calculation called return on capital employed (ROCE) that tells you this. Quality companies have high interest rates, or high ROCEs. You will learn how to calculate ROCE and to understand what it tells you about a company. Once you have read this chapter you will begin to look at shares in a completely different way to many people, and you will be a better investor because of it.

Chapter 3 is all about cash flow. Whilst profits are very important, they are not the same as cash. Quality companies turn a high proportion of their profits into cash. This chapter will introduce you to something called free cash flow and show you how to calculate it and why it matters. You will also learn the reasons why a company may or may not be able to produce free cash flow, and how to separate good free cash flow companies from bad ones.

Chapter 4 is another chapter about cash flow because it is so important. It will show you how to analyse a company's cash flow performance so that you can find out if it is a quality business or not. It will tell you if a company is spending too much money, or not enough, on its business. It will also show you how to spot companies that look like they generate a lot of cash when they don't, and companies that look like they don't generate a lot of cash when they really do. Once you have mastered the skills in this chapter you will know how to thoroughly analyse a company, which will give you an edge over less diligent investors.

1

PROFITS

I<small>N THIS CHAPTER</small> I focus on the most basic, but most important, number in investing – profits. Within this chapter, I look at the following two areas of a company's financial performance:

1. *The history of sales and profits* – this will quickly give you a good idea as to whether a company has been doing well or badly in the past.

2. *Profit margins* – how much of a company's sales are turned into profits. A high profit margin is a hallmark of a quality company.

To understand how profitable a company is, you will have to do some basic calculations. These are known as ratios and they compare one number in a company's financial statements with another one. Ratios provide you with useful information about a company and help you understand it better so that you can make better investment decisions.

All you need is a pen, paper and a calculator to work out the ratios you will come across in this book (although it is quicker and easier to use a spreadsheet). There are also financial software packages that you can subscribe to that will do all this legwork for you in a matter of minutes.

What a quality company looks like

To make this chapter as clear and instructive as possible, I use a real company as an example so that you can see how to work with the right profit numbers in practice.

I've chosen Domino's Pizza UK & Ireland plc (Domino's) as a case study example of a good – some would say a great – company. Domino's has been a very successful company in recent years and it has richly rewarded its shareholders.

NOTE: As mentioned in the Preface, I use Domino's to show you how to analyse a company and find out if it is a good investment throughout the book.

Let's begin by looking at the first aspects of profits I mentioned above: sales and profit history.

1. Sales and profit history

A company makes money by selling its products and services. What you want to see is a company that has been good at selling more every year. When you are looking for great businesses to invest in, an ability to grow is very important.

Sales (also referred to as turnover or revenue) are the lifeblood of any business. They are the source of money flowing into its coffers. Without sales a company is not going to last very long.

So, the first thing to look for is sales, and then growing sales year after year.

However, while growing sales is all well and good, if you are an investor you want to see a company turning those sales into profits. It is quite common to find companies that have sales but no profits as they haven't sold enough to cover all their costs. If you are going to make money from investing in a company over the long haul then it has to be profitable *and* it has to be able to grow those profits in the future.

That's all quite straightforward so far: we are looking for companies that increase their sales over the years and turn those growing sales into growing profits.

The six measures of profit

Despite that being straightforward, there is room for confusion with company profit numbers because there are a few different profit numbers reported by companies, including:

1. Gross profits

2. Trading, or operating, profits

3. Earnings before interest and tax (EBIT)

4. Profit before tax (PBT)

5. Profit after tax (PAT)

6. Earnings per share (EPS)

1. PROFITS

I will clarify this situation in this chapter!

All these profit numbers, as well as a company's revenue (sales), can be found in its income statement, which is part of its annual report. When you are looking at an income statement you will come across different terms such as income, earnings and profit. These all mean the same thing – they are all different words used to describe a form of profit.

Table 1.1 provides an example of what is in a typical income statement, as taken from Domino's 2015 annual report.

Table 1.1: Domino's group income statement

	2015 Total (£'000)	2014 Total (£'000)
Revenue	**316,788**	**288,691**
Cost of sales	(193,171)	(180,202)
Gross profit	**123,617**	**108,489**
Distribution costs	[18,949]	[16,021]
Administrative costs	[33,211]	[31,184]
Profit total	**71,457**	**61,284**
Share of post-tax profits of associates and joint ventures	1,724	1,047
Operating profit	**73,181**	**62,331**
Other gains and losses	-	1,147
Profit before interest and taxation	**73,181**	**63,478**
Finance income	362	620
Finance expense	[380]	[1,996]
Profit before taxation	73,163	62,102
Taxation	[13,874]	[12,745]
Profit for the period from continuing operations	**59,289**	**49,357**
Discontinued operations		
Loss for the period from discontinued operations	[9,626]	[6,619]
Profit for the year attributable to the Company	**49,663**	**42,738**
Earnings per share – diluted (pence)	29.5	25.8

You can see the full detail on page 73 of Domino's 2015 annual report, which is available online. I have used the accounting convention of displaying negative numbers in brackets.

The income statement is your first port of call when you are trying to understand how good or bad a company is and how it has been performing.

A simple but very powerful way of analysing a company's income statement is to compare the numbers for the most recent year with the previous year and calculate the rate of change. This is done by dividing this year's number by last year's, subtracting one, then multiplying by 100 to get a percentage. I have done this for Domino's in Table 1.2.

Table 1.2: Domino's income statement analysis, comparing 2014 to 2015

Domino's (£m)	2015	2014	Change (%)
Revenue	316.8	288.7	9.7%
Gross profit	123.6	108.5	13.9%
Operating profit	73.2	62.3	17.5%
Profit before interest and tax (EBIT)	73.2	63.5	15.3%
Profit before tax	73.2	62.1	17.9%
Profit for the year from continuing operations	59.3	49.4	20.0%
Profit for the year attributable to the company	49.7	42.7	16.4%
Earnings per share from continuing operations (diluted)	35.2	29.6	18.9%

You should always start by looking at the revenue number. Increasing revenue is usually a sign of a healthy business. We can see here that Domino's has increased its revenue by 9.7% over the last year. This is a good sign as it is telling us that its sales are higher, which means demand for its products is growing.

Then you should start looking at the changes in profits that have resulted from the change in revenue. If the business is improving then the change in profits should be the same or more than the change in revenue. As you can see from the table above, this has been the case for Domino's in 2015.

But, as we saw above, there are six different profit numbers an investor can look at. Which profit number should you focus on?

Let's look at each of the numbers in more detail to find out which is most useful.

1. Gross profits

Gross profits are defined as sales less the cost of goods sold. This is supposed to tell you the profits that come from the proceeds of selling a product or service, less the cost of making the product, such as raw materials, rents, wages and advertising.

Gross profit is rarely a useful number because different companies tend to put different expenses into their cost of goods sold figure. Many companies don't want their customers or competitors to see how profitable they really are and so one company's gross profit can look very different to another's, even if they are in the same industry. For example, a company might just put the costs of the stock of goods sold whilst another might also include advertising and distribution costs.

For this reason, you shouldn't place too much emphasis on this profit number. However, *as long as the company's way of calculating it doesn't change from year to year*, you can learn something from looking at the trend from year to year.

Referring to Tables 1 and 2, we can see that Domino's gross profit increased by 13.9% – more than the rate of growth in sales – from £108.5m to £123.6m. This is an encouraging sign because it shows that the company is making more money from selling its products or services. The gap between what it costs to make its products and what it sells them for is getting larger.

2. Trading, or operating, profits

Trading, or operating, profits are the profits a company derives from trading its goods or services. This is calculated by taking the money made from sales and subtracting the costs of goods sold and other costs, such as depreciation on plant and machinery, and general administrative costs.

This profit number is one of the best ways of looking at how good or bad a company is.

Unlike gross profit, where companies can decide what expenses they wish to include when calculating it, operating profits are reliable. The operating profit tells you how much money is left over after all a company's expenses – the costs of stock, wages, depreciation, advertising, etc. – have been deducted from revenues. This makes operating profit a very clean measure of profit that allows the investor to compare changes between years, and compare with other companies.

Another advantage is that operating profit is not affected by how much debt a company has and the interest expenses from that, or the rate of tax paid. These two things can make comparisons more difficult, as I will show later in the book.

Domino's operating profits increased by 17.5% from £62.3m to £73.2m from 2014 to 2015. This is another sign that the company's performance is improving, as this increase is greater than the increase in revenue.

3. Earnings before interest and tax (EBIT)

In many cases EBIT – which Domino's refers to as "profit before interest and tax" – is a very similar number to operating profit, but it also includes the share of profits made from businesses that aren't wholly owned by the company (these are known as associates and joint ventures). You will see the terms *EBIT* or *profit before interest and tax* variously used by different companies. The terms are both referring to the same profit number. I prefer to use the term EBIT because it is used more frequently by companies and financial commentators.

In my opinion, EBIT is the best profit number to use when you are analysing a company. EBIT is my favourite profit number for analysing a company's performance and I use it extensively throughout this book. When I was a professional investment analyst it was the number I spent most time on as I found it the most helpful in understanding how good a company was and ultimately how much its shares were worth.

Let me explain why.

The best way to think about EBIT is that it is a measure of how good the management of a company is at making money from the company's assets. EBIT is stated after all a company's operating costs have been expensed, but before financing expenses such as interest on borrowings and tax.

This distinction is very important and is central to the investment process explained in this book. What we are trying to do in order to become better investors is to identify good businesses to invest in. To do this, you need to have a reliable way of identifying them.

As I will explain in the next chapter, good companies make lots of profits (EBIT) as a percentage of the money that has been invested in them (the value of assets or capital employed). The problem with using measures of profit such as profit before tax (PBT) or profit after tax is that these profit numbers become distorted by how a company's assets are financed and how much tax is paid.

This is best illustrated by an example.

John and his friend Bob have decided to become landlords. They buy identical houses next door to each other, each costing £100,000. John decides to pay for all £100,000 of his house with money from his savings. This amount of his own money that John puts into the purchase is John's *equity* in the deal. Bob doesn't have much savings. So he buys his house with £5000 of his own money (this £5000 is Bob's equity in the deal) and borrows £95,000 from a bank by getting a mortgage. The mortgage has an interest rate of 5%.

They soon get tenants to rent their houses and both charge the same amount of rent. After they have incurred some costs for keeping the houses well maintained they both have EBIT of £10,000 after their first year in business.

John and Bob meet up in the pub to discuss how well they have done and show each other their income statements for their first year in business. These income statements are shown in Table 1.3.

Table 1.3: Income statements from John's and Bob's rental businesses

Income statement (£)	John	Bob
EBIT (A)	10,000	10,000
Interest @ 5%	0	–4750
Profit before tax	10,000	5250
Taxation @ 20%	–2000	–1050
Profit for the year (B)	8000	4200
Value of House (assets) (C)	100,000	100,000
Mortgage	0	95,000
Savings invested (Equity) (D)	100,000	5000
Total invested (equity + borrowings)	100,000	100,000
Return on assets (A/C)	10%	10%
Return on equity (B/D)	8%	84%

John says that he has made more money as he has £8000 after tax, compared with Bob who only has £4200 (as you can see in the row 'Profit for the year (B)'). Bob says that he has done better than John. This is because he has only put £5000 of his own money into the house and has made profits of £4200 – a return of 84%.

The truth is that they have both done as well as each other. They have each made £10,000 of EBIT on a £100,000 house (which you can see in the row 'Profit before tax'). They are both getting a 10% return on their investment. The fact that Bob has financed his house with borrowed money massively distorts matters. By focusing on EBIT you can avoid these problems and see that both houses are of equal quality in investment terms.

That's not to say that debts and taxes don't matter. They matter a lot. However, when it comes to identifying good businesses they do not matter and they can cause you to make mistakes. Where they matter is in identifying risky businesses, which we will look at in Part 2.

Getting back to Domino's (Table 1.2), we can see that EBIT increased by 15.3% to £73.2m from 2014 to 2015. Again, this is faster than the growth in revenues which suggests that its business performance is improving.

4. Profit before tax (PBT)

Profit before tax (PBT) is a company's EBIT plus any interest income received, less any interest on borrowings paid (known as net interest).

This is the profit number that many professional analysts and the media focus on. Whilst it is not a trivial number, it is not as useful as EBIT because it is affected by how much debt a company has and the interest bill associated with this.

For example, you can have two companies with an identical EBIT but if one has lots of debt and the other has none, the debt-free company will have a higher PBT. This can make comparing companies' PBT figures difficult, as we saw in the John and Bob mortgage example above.

In general, lower interest bills are better than higher ones as it means more of the company's trading profits or EBIT can flow into shareholders' pockets.

Domino's PBT increased by 17.9% to £73.2m from 2014 to 2015. It has virtually no net interest expense.

5. Profit after tax (PAT)

Profit after tax (PAT) is a company's PBT less a deduction for taxation.

Companies usually have to pay corporation tax on their profits. From April 2017, the rate of UK corporation tax is 19%. If a company has taxable profits outside the UK it will pay a different tax rate on them. You can work out a company's individual tax rate by dividing the taxation expense in the income statement by the company's pre-tax profit figure. This is known as the company's effective tax rate.

company effective tax rate = taxation/pre-tax profit

Domino's effective tax rate in 2015 was therefore: 13874/73163 = 18.96%

This is very close to the 20% statutory rate of corporation tax in the UK at the time, but you will find that very few companies pay exactly the statutory rate on their pre-tax profits.

This is because the pre-tax profits they report to investors and the ones they report to the tax authorities (HMRC) can be different. For example, some expenses such as money spent on new plant and equipment receive favourable tax treatment and reduce a company's taxable profits in the eyes of the tax authorities, and therefore the amount of tax payable. Other expenses are not deductible for tax purposes, which means the company's profits can be higher in the eyes of the tax authorities and it therefore has to pay more tax.

If you are looking at a UK company that trades exclusively in the UK then there is a rough rule of thumb that tends to hold:

If the effective tax rate is greater than the statutory rate of UK corporation tax, then a company's profits in the eyes of HMRC are higher than those that are being reported to investors. If the effective rate is lower, then profits reported to HMRC tend to be lower than those reported to investors.

You need to be wary of companies with very low effective tax rates. This is because the reason for keeping them low may not last forever. A company will usually comment on why its effective tax rate is lower than the statutory rate in the finance director's review, which will be found in the company's annual report. Below is an excerpt from construction company Severfield's annual report explaining its lower effective rate in 2016.

> "The underlying tax charge of GBP2.3m (2015: GBP1.4m) represents an effective tax rate of 17 per cent on the applicable profit (which excludes results from JVs and associates). This is consistent with an effective tax rate of 17 per cent in the prior year, reflecting an unchanged UK statutory corporation tax rate of 20 per cent over the same period. The Group's effective tax rate is lower than the UK statutory rate primarily due to the continued recognition of deferred tax assets on losses which arose in prior periods." – Severfield plc Annual Report 2016

This suggests that when the benefit of those losses have been used up, Severfield's effective tax rate will almost certainly increase.

It is also important to note that the number for taxation that you see in a company's income statement is rarely the same as the amount of cash handed over to the government (which is shown in the company's cash flow statement), as some taxes don't have to be paid immediately (known as deferred taxes).

Tax is a very complicated subject. All you need to know is that different companies pay different amounts of tax and this means that comparing companies based on their PAT figures is difficult.

As far as Domino's is concerned, the most important figure to look at here is the profit after tax from continuing activities. This number excludes businesses that have been closed or sold during the year and gives the investor a better way of judging the company's progress in future years.

Domino's PAT on this basis increased by 20% to £59.3m from 2014 to 2015. It was helped by the fact that its tax bill only increased by 8.8% – from £12.7m to £13.9m – during the year.

6. Earnings per share (EPS)

Earnings per share (EPS) is one of the most used and abused numbers in finance. It can be calculated in many different ways, which makes it very confusing for investors.

The most basic calculation is to take a company's PAT and then subtract any profits that belong to minority interests and preferred shareholders, and divide by the weighted average number of shares in issue throughout the year.

A rising EPS does not necessarily mean a good company. Many companies boost EPS by shrinking the number of shares in issue by buying back their own shares, rather than by growing profits. EPS does have its uses to investors but it is not a good measure of company performance.

If you are going to look at EPS then it is best to look at diluted EPS. This looks at the impact on EPS that will be caused by additional shares – such as share options, share bonuses or debt that converts into shares – being issued in the future.

The important takeaway from the discussion of the six profit measures is that EBIT is the best profit number to use. We will concentrate on EBIT from here onwards.

The ten-year EBIT view

When you are looking at a company's financial performance using EBIT, you should look over a period of at least ten years, as this is sufficient to take into account different parts of an economic cycle. You want to get a feel for whether the company has been able to prosper in good economic times and bad ones as well.

Your first step is to access the company's accounts and find the EBIT figures for the past ten years. When you have these, you should display them in a table or a chart to enable you to see the pattern over the last ten years.

I have done this for Domino's in Figure 1.1. As we can see in the chart, Domino's has been very successful in growing its sales and profits (EBIT) over the last ten years. The reason that I have included sales in the chart as well as profits is so I can check that the growth in profits is coming from selling more, which is what I want to see.

It is possible to grow EBIT by cutting costs rather than growing sales. The problem with this is that the scope to cut costs eventually runs out, which makes it a poor long-term source of profit growth. You should generally avoid companies which grow mainly by cutting costs.

If you are investigating a company and you see a result like that of Domino's for EBIT, this is a very positive sign and you should investigate the company further.

For Figure 1.1, I used a profit figure known as normalised EBIT, which ignores any one-off gains and costs incurred during the year. These one-off gains and costs are known as exceptional items. They are not expected to recur every year and are excluded from the calculation of a company's normalised or underlying profits.

This gives a more accurate measure of a company's true underlying profitability. Where possible, you should use a company's normalised EBIT figures.

Figure 1.1: Domino's growing sales and EBIT for 2006–2015

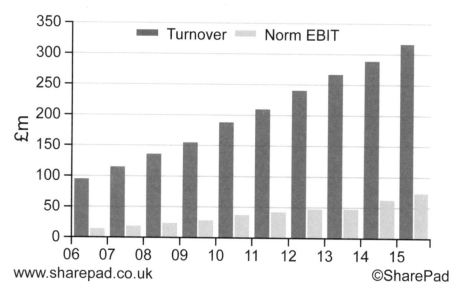

www.sharepad.co.uk   ©SharePad

Normalised EBIT

However, bear in mind that companies can abuse the use of exceptional costs and classify them as one-off when they actually occur in most years. They do this to boost their normalised profits, which most professional investors look at. A good example of this is redundancy costs. If you come across a company with significant exceptional costs every year – and therefore a big gap between reported and normalised profits – it may be a sign of aggressive accounting. Companies with aggressive accounting often make very bad investments and you should stay away from them.

An example of the difference between a company's reported EBIT – which contains all one-off costs and gains – and the normalised EBIT can be seen with Domino's in 2013, as shown in Table 1.4. Note that the row 'Profit before interest and taxation' is EBIT.

Domino's 2013 income contained £27.5m of one-off expenses (related to its German business) and £1.7m of one-off gains relating to a profit from selling investments. You can see this in the rows for 'Administrative costs' and 'Profit on the sale of investments'. This meant that its normalised EBIT was £25.8m higher than its total EBIT (£47.9m versus £22.1m).

Table 1.4: Domino's group income statement, 52 weeks ended 29 December 2013

	Before exceptional items £000	Exceptional items £000	Total £000
Revenue	268,902	-	268,902
Cost of sales	[171,954]	-	[171,954]
Gross profit	96,948	-	96,948
Distribution costs	[15,704]	-	[15,704]
Administrative costs	[33,970]	[27,520]	[61,490]
	47,274	[27,520]	19,754
Share of post-tax profits of associates and joint ventures	642	-	642
Operating profit	47,916	[27,520]	20,396
Profit on the sale of investments	-	1,745	1,745
Profit before interest and taxation [EBIT]	47,916	[25,775]	22,141
Finance income	789	-	789
Finance expense	[1,104]	[236]	[1,340]
Profit before taxation	47,601	[26,011]	21,590
Taxation	[10,089]	622	[9,467]
Profit for the period	37,512	[25,389]	12,123
Profit for the period attributable to:			
Owners of the parent			17,568
Non-controlling interests			5,445
			12,123
Earnings per share (post-exceptional items)			
– Basic (pence)			10.7
– Diluted (pence)			10.7
Earnings per share (pre-exceptional items)			
– Basic (pence)			24.0
– Diluted (pence)			23.9

You should be wary of companies which have regular one-off expenses and where normalised EBIT is always significantly higher than total EBIT. This is telling you that these costs are not really one-offs, but regular. This can be a sign of aggressive accounting and is often a signal to steer well clear of a company. Domino's EBIT numbers are fairly close together most of the time, as illustrated in Figure 1.2. This is a good sign.

Figure 1.2: Comparing Domino's EBIT and normalised EBIT figures for 2006–2015

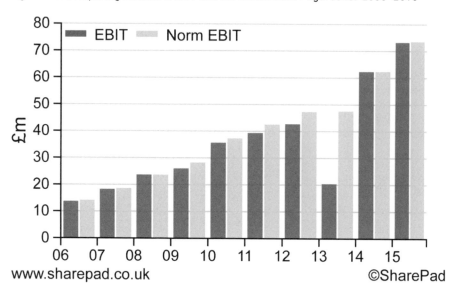

www.sharepad.co.uk   ©SharePad

In summary, when you start out to analyse a company you should find out whether it produced growing sales and growing normalised EBIT over a period of the last ten years. Reported EBIT and normalised EBIT should also be roughly the same in most years. If you can find such a company, then it is a good sign that it is a quality company.

But of course we don't stop there. Looking at a company's sales and profit history is your first step in analysing a company, but it is not sufficient on its own. To learn enough to make an investment decision about a company's shares you need to do a bit more work by moving on to look at its profit margin.

2. Profit margin

A company's level of profit (EBIT) tells you only so much – you need to do some calculations to find out more.

One of the important numbers that you should calculate is a company's EBIT margin, which you might otherwise refer to as its profit margin. This is the proportion of the business' sales that are turned into EBIT, expressed as a percentage. The equation to calculate EBIT margin is as follows:

EBIT margin = EBIT/sales × 100%

High profit margins are generally better than low profit margins. The reason for this is that higher profit margin companies are better placed to withstand temporary periods of difficulty which might depress their profits. A company with a 15% profit margin would still be very profitable if margins fell to 10%. A company with a 3% profit margin might see its profits completely wiped out with a similar 5 percentage point drop in profit margin.

High profit margins therefore combine the characteristics of quality and safety, which are two of the most important things you are looking for in a potential investment.

Generally speaking, I look for companies with a minimum profit margin of 10%–15%. This quickly narrows down a list of qualifying companies to look at. Additionally, I want to see that a company has been able to generate high profit margins consistently over time. This allows me to ignore companies where profits are temporarily and unsustainably high, and helps me avoid more risky investments.

Different businesses and sectors have different profit margins. Table 1.5 provides a list of companies and their sectors to show you a range of company profit margins. It is generally not important what sector a company operates in. All you need to be sure of is that the margins have been consistently high and stand a good chance of staying that way.

Table 1.5: High margin FTSE 100 companies

Name	EBIT margin	Sector
Hargreaves Lansdown	56.2	Financial Services
Land Securities Group	48.6	Real Estate Investment Trusts
United Utilities Group	41.8	Gas, Water & Multiutilities
InterContinental Hotels Group	36.6	Travel & Leisure
British American Tobacco	35.2	Tobacco
Shire	34.1	Pharmaceuticals & Biotechnology
Schroders	29.2	Financial Services
Severn Trent	29.0	Gas, Water & Multiutilities
BHP Billiton	28.1	Mining

Name	EBIT margin	Sector
Diageo	27.6	Beverages
Reckitt Benckiser Group	26.8	Household Goods & Home Construction
Sage Group (The)	26.4	Software & Computer Services
Worldpay Group	26.2	Support Services
ITV	25.9	Media
Croda International	24.5	Chemicals
Persimmon	21.7	Household Goods & Home Construction
BT Group	20.8	Fixed Line Telecommunications

Source: SharePad

Table 1.6: Lower margin FTSE 100 companies

Name	EBIT margin	Sector
Compass Group	7.3	Travel & Leisure
Kingfisher	7.0	General Retailers
GKN	6.7	Automobiles & Parts
Capita	6.7	Support Services
CRH	6.4	Construction & Materials
Wolseley	6.0	Support Services
Centrica	6.0	Gas, Water & Multiutilities
Bunzl	6.0	Support Services
TUI	5.1	Travel & Leisure
Dixons Carphone	4.5	General Retailers
Johnson Matthey	4.0	Chemicals
Royal Mail Group	3.5	Industrial Transportation
Sainsbury (J)	2.9	Food & Drug Retailers

Source: SharePad

Again, as for EBIT, it is useful to view a company's EBIT margin over a period of the last ten years. What you are looking for in a great business is consistently high profit margins, or even better a trend of rising profit margins, over a ten-year period. If a company can regularly turn a large chunk of its sales into profits that is usually a sign of a very good business. The fact that it has been able to do this for a reasonable length of time may also be telling you that the company has been able to see off competitive threats as well as cope with the ups and downs of an economic cycle.

To help me visualise a company's ten-year profit margin performance, I display this in a chart. I have done this for Domino's in Figure 1.3. As we can see, Domino's has high profit margins across this period. Apart from a small blip in 2013, profit margins have been consistently high and have increased significantly for the last two years it has reported.

Figure 1.3: Domino's EBIT margin for 2006–2015

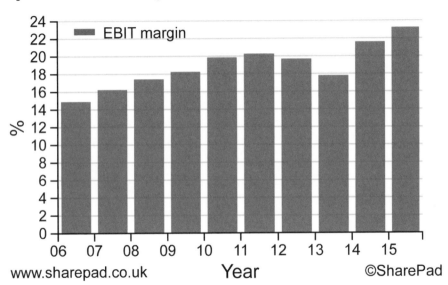

Now that we have established the usefulness of EBIT as a profit measure, we can put it to even better use by using it to work out whether a company is producing a high interest rate on the money it invests. I'll show you how to do this in the next chapter.

2

A COMPANY'S INTEREST RATE

PROFIT MARGINS ARE usually a reliable indicator of a good or bad business. But like sales and profits, on their own they do not tell you the whole story. That's because the profit margin does not tell you anything about how much money a company spent to produce its sales and profits. If a company is growing its sales and profits, the investor needs to know how it is doing this.

The best way for a company to grow is to sell more without having to spend more. Not many companies can do this. In order to grow, companies usually have to invest in new assets which will allow them to produce more. Companies also buy other companies in order to grow. Both of these methods of expanding the business cost money and the investor needs to take account of the amount of money spent in order to get a realistic view of a company's sales and profits.

To really find out how good a company is you need to work out whether it is getting a decent bang for its buck. Is the company getting a good return in sales and profit growth for the amount it is investing to produce that growth? How much profit is the company getting as a percentage of the total amount of money invested in it? I refer to the return a company earns on the money it invests as the company's *interest rate*.

In other words, just as you assess bank savings accounts by looking at the rate of interest they offer, you can do the same with companies and work out a company's interest rate. The higher this interest rate, the better the business tends to be.

One of the best ways to work out a company's interest rate is to calculate a ratio known as return on capital employed (ROCE). ROCE is a great way for investors to identify high-quality companies. I look for companies that have been able to consistently generate ROCE of 15% or more. This chapter will show you how to calculate and interpret a company's ROCE.

NOTE: It is important not to confuse this discussion of a company's interest rate with the return the investor will receive on their investment in the company. When I refer to the company's interest rate, I am talking about the return the company makes on the money invested in its projects.

Return on capital employed (ROCE)

The return on capital employed is calculated as follows:

ROCE = EBIT/capital employed × 100%

I don't really like the term *capital employed*, as it seems abstruse. I much prefer the simple term *money invested*. That is all capital employed really means.

What we are really working out here is the company's return on the money it has invested.

So, how do you work out the amount of money a company has invested?

Capital employed – or money invested

Let's return to the simple example we used in the previous chapter of a landlord buying a house.

A landlord buys a house for £100,000 with a £95,000 mortgage and £5000 of savings. Another way of saying this is that in spending £5000 of his savings on the purchase, the landlord has put £5000 of equity into the deal. Here, there are two ways to work out the amount of money invested:

1. The price of the house, which is £100,000. Here we are looking at the value of assets bought.

2. The amount of savings and borrowings used to buy the house. In this case, the £95,000 mortgage and £5000 of savings, which gives the same value of £100,000. Here we are looking at the value of money invested.

The same principles apply to companies. You can calculate the money invested in a company from either the asset side or the liability side of a company's balance sheet.

Let's do this for Domino's Pizza. Its balance sheet is shown in Table 2.1.

2. A COMPANY'S INTEREST RATE

Table 2.1: Domino's balance sheet

	At 27 December 2015 £000	At 28 December 2014 (restated) £000
Non-current assets		
Intangible assets	12,000	10,561
Property, plant and equipment	58,566	57,374
Prepaid operating lease charges	1,010	1,072
Trade and other receivables	7,107	5,618
Net investment in finance leases	1,209	1,285
Investments in associates and joint ventures	7,985	7,170
Deferred tax asset	7,851	8,507
	95,728	91,587
Current assets		
Inventories	6,208	4,826
Prepaid operating lease charges	194	198
Trade and other receivables	28,747	34,735
Net investment in finance leases	774	900
Cash and cash equivalents	52,860	33,743
Assets classified as held for sale	935	-
	89,718	74,402
Total assets	**185,446**	**165,989**
Current liabilities		
Trade and other payables	[52,912]	[47,523]
Deferred income	[4,312]	[4,584]
Financial liabilities	[988]	[16,054]
Deferred and contingent consideration	[2,865]	[3,481]
Current tax liabilities	[4,151]	[5,072]
Provisions	[6,113]	[1,270]
	[71,341]	[78,344]
Non-current liabilities		
Trade and other payables	[316]	-
Financial liabilities	[11,450]	[6,731]
Deferred income	[3,334]	[2,938]
Deferred and contingent consideration	-	[2,483]

	At 27 December 2015 £000	At 28 December 2014 (restated) £000
Deferred tax liabilities	[115]	[95]
Provisions	[1,215]	[2,000]
Total liabilities	**[87,771]**	**[92,591]**
Net assets	**97,675**	**73,398**
Shareholders' equity		
Called up share capital	2,606	2,592
Share premium account	29,155	25,597
Capital redemption reserve	425	425
Capital reserve - own shares	[2,238]	[2,238]
Currency translation reserve	[280]	572
Retained earnings	68,007	46,450
Total equity shareholders' funds	**97,675**	**73,398**

Starting with the asset side, we take the company's total assets at the end of 2015, which were £185.4m (see the row 'Total assets'). We then subtract a figure for its non-interest-bearing current liabilities, such as trade creditors (bills that are outstanding at the end of the year), accruals (for example bills such as rent or telephone bills that are paid in arrears but have been partly used) and tax due.

These non-interest-bearing current liabilities are taken away from total assets because they are a form of interest-free credit which reduces the amount of money a company needs to invest. For example, Domino's owes its suppliers (row 'Trade and other payables') £52.91m at the end of 2015. These costs have been expensed in calculating profits but have not been paid at the end of the year. Had they been, then Domino's would have £52.91m less cash, or £52.91m more debt, than it had at the end of the year. This would have meant it would have had to invest that amount more (capital) in its business. Instead, by giving it time to pay its bills (a form of credit), Domino's suppliers are effectively financing part of its business for it. This is why we deduct non-interest bearing current liabilities from total assets to calculate a company's capital employed.

In 2015, Domino's amount of non-interest-bearing current liabilities was £70.3m (£71.3m of current liabilities less financial liabilities of £0.988m). The quickest way to get to the figure for non-interest-bearing current liabilities is to find the number for current liabilities and remove the amount of short-term borrowings from this. The short-term borrowings on Domino's balance sheet above is labelled financial liabilities, totalling £988,000. Companies will also refer to this as short-term borrowings or the current portion of total borrowings.

This means you can calculate a company's capital employed or money invested with just three figures:

capital employed = total assets − current liabilities + short-term borrowings

As you can see, short-term borrowings are removed from current liabilities by adding back short-term borrowings after current liabilities have been subtracted.

So, Domino's total capital employed at the end of 2015 was £185.4m minus £71.3m plus £1m, or £115.1m. The figure for 2014 was £103.8m. We can see that the amount of money invested in the company has increased by £11.3m from 2014 to 2015.

What I have done here is calculate capital employed from the assets side. As mentioned above, it is also possible to calculate capital employed by looking at liabilities and equity. We can calculate money invested from the liability and equity side of the balance sheet as follows:

capital employed = total borrowings + other long-term liabilities + total equity

For Domino's, this works out as: total borrowings (£1.0m + £11.4m), plus other long-term liabilities (£5m), plus total equity of (£97.7m) = £115.1m. This is the same number as we calculated above with the assets method.

The total borrowings number is calculated by taking the financial liabilities figures from current liabilities of £988,000 and £11,450,000 from non-current liabilities. Added together this gives £12.43m of total borrowings.

Other long-term liabilities are trade and other payables (£316,000), deferred income (£3.334m), deferred tax (£115,000) and provisions (£1.215m). This gives a total of £4.98m.

Total equity of £97.675m is found right at the bottom of the balance sheet.

You can see where I am getting the numbers to do these calculations in Domino's balance sheet in Table 2.1.

A note on cash balances

Some people like to take away the value of cash from total assets to reduce capital employed even further. They argue that this cash can be used to pay off liabilities such as borrowings and reduce the amount of money that needs to be invested in the business.

This might be true, but as a company outsider you don't know if it is. A company might have cash sitting in its bank account on the last day of its financial year – when the balance sheet is calculated – because it delayed paying a supplier until the following day. That cash is not free for the company to do with as it pleases – it has to be used to pay a bill in the future.

By including cash as part of capital employed/money invested you are being more conservative. It is a good practice to be as conservative as possible when analysing a company, as it is better to err on the side of caution rather than make a company look better than it really is.

NOTE: When you are calculating any ratio over a period of years you need to make sure that you are using the same numbers for each and every year so that comparisons are meaningful.

Using average capital employed

Ideally, you would like to know the amount of money a company has invested throughout the year, rather than at a frozen point in time when the financial statements were compiled. This is not possible because a balance sheet only gives the figures for the last day of a company's financial year.

This is problematic, for example, because if a company spent a lot of money on new assets on the last day of the year this would be included on its balance sheet, even though it would not yet have produced any profits from this investment in new assets. This would have the effect of reducing a company's ROCE, distorting the figure and failing to give a true picture.

To limit this problem, ROCE is usually calculated using a company's average capital employed over a period of two years. For Domino's, we would take the figures for 2015 and 2014 and divide by two. This would give a figure of £109.5m ((£115.1m + £103.8m)/2 = £109.5m).

We can now use this to calculate Domino's ROCE.

ROCE = EBIT/capital employed × 100%

Domino's has normalised EBIT of £73.6m[1] for 2015, so Domino's ROCE for 2015 would be:

---

1   I'm using numbers from SharePad investment software which are normalised and, in this case, they are almost identical to the company's underlying numbers. If you refer back to pages 13–15 where I calculated Domino's EBIT, you can see this figure of £73.6m is very close to the £73.2m calculated there.

(£73.6m/£109.5m) × 100 = 67%

That is a very impressive number. This means that Domino's is returning 67% on the money it invests in its business. In general, a ROCE which is consistently over 20% is a sign of a high-quality company.

If we look at Domino's ROCE over the last ten years in Figure 2.1, we can see that it has been consistently very high. From 2009 to 2014 it declined quite significantly, which might have been a sign that the company's best days were behind it (or it was investing heavily to grow profits in the future). But then in 2014 and 2015 ROCE returned to the heights it was at back in 2008.

Figure 2.1: Domino's ROCE for 2006–2015

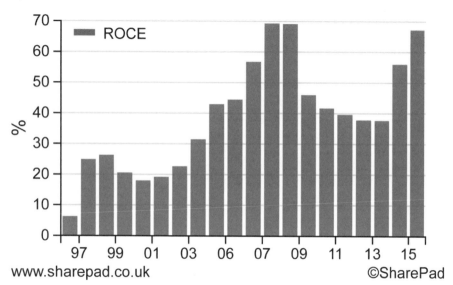

Thinking about ROCE in more detail

Effectively what this ROCE of 67% means is that for every £100 Domino's invests, it returns £67. At least, that is what seems to be happening.

I say *seems*, because when you come across a ROCE number as high as this you have to ask yourself if it really is as good as it seems? For example, has Domino's really invested only £115.1m when it has hundreds of pizza shops across the UK?

The answer in reality is, no, it hasn't. The company has rented or leased most of its pizza shops and has signed up to pay rent for many years into the future. These shops and the obligations to pay rent are not on Domino's balance sheet.

(Note: From 2019 onwards a new accounting standard will make companies put these obligations to pay rents on their balance sheets.) However, if Domino's had bought the shops with a bank loan the assets and liabilities involved would be there on the balance sheet. This situation is true of most high street retailers and it is something to be aware of.

By renting rather than owning its shops, Domino's is actually understating its assets and liabilities and therefore the amount of money it has invested in the business, or its capital employed, because due to accounting practices these data are not shown on the balance sheet when the properties are not owned by the company. To get a truer view of its real ROCE, we need to make a few adjustments to the ROCE calculations for these rented shops.

How to calculate a rent- or lease-adjusted ROCE

In my opinion, this calculation is one of the most powerful and underused in financial analysis. It is quite advanced analysis, but it should not frighten you. It isn't really that complicated, despite its immense value to the investor. By calculating a lease-adjusted ROCE, you are getting a truer picture of how profitable a business really is. It is a number that will help you identify very good companies and keep you away from ones that might look good but aren't in reality.

You should calculate a lease-adjusted ROCE for every company you look at. For some sectors such as airlines, retailers and train operators it is vital that you do so, as these are businesses that have huge amounts of rented assets.

If you do this you will be doing something that very few professional investors even bother with. This is a way that you can get an analytical edge which can improve your investment results. (See Appendix 1 at the end of the book for an example that shows how using the lease-adjusted ROCE can produce stunning results.)

To calculate a lease-adjusted ROCE, you first need to estimate the value of the rented shops that would be on Domino's balance sheet if it had bought them outright. You then need to add this estimate to the previous calculation of capital employed, which didn't include this adjustment.

To do this you need to know how much the company was spending on rent during the year. You can find this in a note to the accounts in the latest annual report, under the heading 'operating lease payments'. You can see this in Table 2.2.

The simplest way to estimate the value of the shops that are rented is to multiply the annual rental and lease expense by a number between 6 and 8. This is how the credit rating agencies such as Moody's and Standard & Poor's do it and how many professional investment analysts do it as well.

2. A COMPANY'S INTEREST RATE

Table 2.2: Domino's note to the accounts for 2015, including 'operating lease payments'

	52 weeks ended 27 December 2015, £000	52 weeks ended 28 December 2014, £000
– land and buildings	18,352	17,938
– plant, machinery and vehicles	2,961	2,936
Total operating lease payments	**21,313**	**20,874**

See page 88 of Domino's 2015 accounts for the full details.

I've multiplied this £21.3m of rent expenses by 7 to get an estimated value of £149.1m if the assets were owned instead of leased. You then add this to the previous calculation of capital employed. So we take our previous 2015 capital employed figure of £115.1m and add £149.1m to get an adjusted capital employed figure of £264.2m.

Once this is done, you also have to adjust Domino's profits.

This is because the rent expense of £21.3m is largely made up of two costs: an interest cost (as leases are essentially a form of borrowing) and other costs associated with the assets being rented.

As you need a pre-interest measure of profit (EBIT) to calculate ROCE, you need to add an estimate of interest in the lease payment back to Domino's existing EBIT (remember that the existing EBIT is £73.6m). To keep things simple, I've assumed an interest rate of 7%.

£149.1m × 7% = £10.4m

This gives a lease-adjusted EBIT of £84m (£73.6m + £10.4m). To calculate Domino's lease-adjusted ROCE, we take its lease-adjusted EBIT and divide it by its lease-adjusted average capital employed.

To do this we need to calculate the lease-adjusted capital employed for 2014 as well. We already know the unadjusted figure of £103.8m from earlier. Now we take the operating lease expense for the year of £20,874m (see Table 2.2) and multiply it by 7 to get an estimated value of rented assets of £146.1m. Add this figure to unadjusted £103.8m to get an adjusted capital employed figure for 2014 of £249.9m.

Average adjusted capital employed is therefore £257.1m ((£264.2m + £249.9m)/2) and our adjusted ROCE is:

£84m/£257.1m = 32.7%

The adjusted ROCE is still a very impressive number.

I have also calculated Domino's lease-adjusted ROCE for the six years from 2010–2015 and the data is presented in Table 2.3.

Table 2.3 Domino's lease-adjusted ROCE for 2010–2015

£m unless stated	2010	2011	2012	2013	2014	2015
Rental & lease	14.7	16.2	17.5	19.5	20.9	21.3
Capitalised leases	102.8	113.1	122.3	136.8	146.1	149.2
Lease-adj capital employed	200.1	230.5	255.4	255.8	249.8	264.3
Lease interest	7.2	7.9	8.6	9.6	10.2	10.4
Norm EBIT	37.4	42.5	47.3	47.5	62.4	73.6
Lease-adj EBIT (7x,7%)	44.5%	50.5%	55.9%	57.1%	72.6%	84.0%
Lease-adj ROCE (7x,7%)	23.8%	23.4%	23.0%	22.3%	28.7%	32.7%

Source: SharePad

Figure 2.2 shows the lease-adjusted ROCE for the ten years from 2006–2015. As you can see, lease-adjusted ROCE was consistently over 20% and increased significantly in the last two years. Based on this historic trend, we can safely assume that we are looking at a very impressive company.

I'll have more to say on the subject of rents in Chapter 11 on hidden debts.

For now, we move on to how to take the ROCE and turn it into even more useful information by using a method called DuPont analysis.

Figure 2.2: Domino's lease-adjusted ROCE for 2006–2015

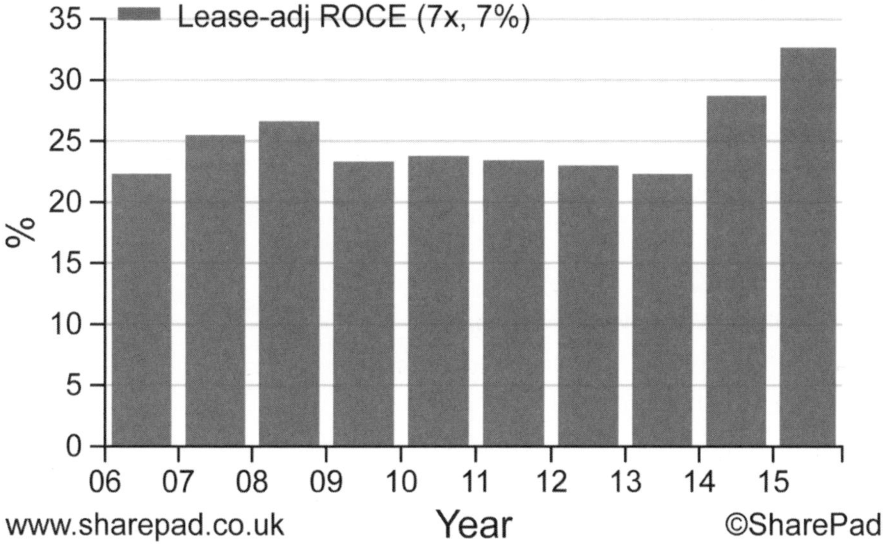

DuPont analysis

To gain an even better understanding of how a company generates its ROCE, you can do something called a DuPont analysis. This can really help you understand how a company makes its profits. Again, it is not complicated, but it is also an underused tool of analysis. It is another way for you to get an analytical edge over less diligent investors. The reason why it is so useful is that it shows you how sustainable a company's profitability might be and how it might improve or get worse in the future.

DuPont analysis is one of the simplest and most powerful ways to analyse a company's financial performance. I use it extensively when researching my own investments because it allows me to quickly focus on the most important bits of information about a company. It helps me understand a company better and focus my research efforts.

This technique was devised by Donaldson Brown in 1919 when he worked for the US chemical company DuPont. Brown broke down a company's ROCE into its constituent parts. In very simple terms, ROCE is the product of a company's profit margins (what proportion of sales turns into profit) and capital turnover (how much in sales is produced per £1 of capital invested). Therefore:

ROCE = profit margin × capital turnover

Just to prove that this is true, I've laid out the calculations for these three ratios below. A bit of basic school maths means that the sales figure on the bottom of the profit margin calculation and on the top of capital turnover calculation cancel each other out when the two ratios are multiplied.

$$\frac{EBIT}{Capital\ employed} = \frac{EBIT}{\cancel{Sales}} \times \frac{\cancel{Sales}}{Capital\ employed}$$

ROCE is determined by two elements

Using Donaldson Brown's ROCE calculation above, we can see that essentially a company's ROCE is affected by two things:

1. What's happening with profit margins.

2. Sales generated per £1 of money invested (capital turnover).

I spend my time thinking about how these are determined and how they might change in the future. Let's look at profit margins first.

1. Profit margins

Profit margins are determined by many different factors. The bigger the gap between revenue coming into the company (the prices of all goods and services sold multiplied by the quantity sold) and costs, the bigger the profit margin.

The key influences on profit margins are:

- *Prices*: Higher prices can boost margins.

- *Costs*: Particularly important is the split between fixed costs (costs that have to be paid regardless of the level of sales, such as rent and most wages) and variable costs (costs which vary with sales, such as raw materials). Companies with a high proportion of fixed costs can see their margins change rapidly in response to small changes in turnover via a process known as *operational gearing*.

- *Mix of products*: Some sales are more profitable than others. A car dealer will make little profit on selling a new car but will make lots of profit on selling services and spare parts. Domino's may sell more sophisticated pizzas at a higher price for its most profitable sales.

- *Volume sold*: Selling more products can boost margins where the company has a high proportion of fixed costs (i.e. high operational gearing). This process can also work in reverse and is clearly seen in manufacturing companies. For example, an industrial plant will have costs related to buildings and machinery, energy, raw materials and wages. Most of these costs are fixed and the company needs to sell a large amount of goods to cover them and break even. Once past break even, the fixed costs are spread over a larger amount of sales, which allows profits to increase rapidly. However, a sharp fall in sales pushes the company back towards break even and possibly into a loss if income cannot cover all the fixed costs.

What we are trying to do here is understand the business behind the profit margin numbers. Profit margins which fluctuate over a period of time are a tell-tale indicator of a cyclical business (where sales move up and down in line with the general economy) and possibly one with high operational gearing. These businesses are more risky and their shares tend not to make suitable long-term investments. This is why stable profit margins are such a desirable characteristic of a business.

You should spend time reading a company's annual report to see if it has anything to say about profit margins. Pay particular attention to any mention of changes in prices, sales mix and volume changes. High-quality companies grow by selling more (volume) and not just by charging more. A company which increases prices but does not increase sales is showing that its customers are responding to the price rise by buying less from them. This may be a sign of trouble ahead and may lead to stagnating or lower profits in the future.

2. Capital turnover

Capital turnover looks at how effectively a company is spending its money to produce sales. A company can increase capital turnover by adopting some of these measures:

- Boosting sales with new products.

- Reducing money invested.

- Cutting working capital by holding less stock of finished goods, getting customers to pay their bills faster and paying suppliers later.

- Cutting the amount of money invested in new assets (capital expenditure, or capex), reducing spending on new assets or increasing efficiency by getting more sales for less investment.

- Getting rid of underperforming assets that have low capital turnover and low ROCE.

Let's have a look at how Domino's stacks up with this type of analysis.

DuPont analysis of Domino's

In Table 2.4 I present the information needed from Domino's accounts in order to perform a DuPont analysis and then show the results in a chart in Figure 2.3 so that you can see how the company's ROCE has evolved over time.

Table 2.4: Domino's DuPont analysis data for 2010–2015

£m unless stated	2010	2011	2012	2013	2014	2015
Turnover	188.1	209.9	240.5	266.8	288.7	316.8
EBIT	44.5	50.5	55.9	57.1	72.6	84.0
Lease-adjusted avg. cap. employed	187.3	215.3	242.9	255.6	252.8	257.1
EBIT margin (%)	23.7%	24.0%	23.2%	21.4%	25.2%	26.5%
Capital turnover (x)	1.0	1.0	1.0	1.0	1.1	1.2
Lease-adjusted ROCE	23.8%	23.4%	23.0%	22.3%	28.7%	32.7%

Source: SharePad

Figure 2.3: Domino's lease-adjusted ROCE, lease-adjusted EBIT margin and lease-adjusted capital turnover for 2005–2015

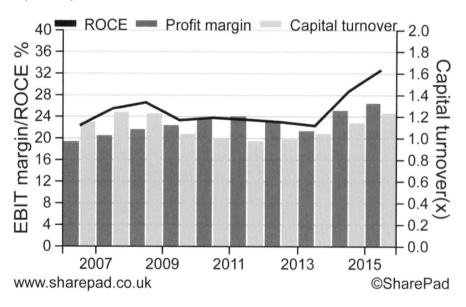

As you can see, from 2010 to 2013 ROCE declined slightly. Domino's was consistently getting £1 of sales for every £1 of capital employed (its turnover and capital employed were similar numbers), but its profit margins were falling.

From 2013, Domino's capital turnover improved to 1.2, which means £1.20 of sales for every £1 invested, whilst profit margins increased significantly from 21.4% to 26.5%. ROCE made a significant leap forward from 22.3% to 32.7%.

Capital turnover versus profit margins

Selling more for each £1 invested (capital turnover) is a good sign and is a good way to improve ROCE. But we also know from the DuPont analysis that a big part of improvement in ROCE comes from improving profit margins.

To add some more clarity to DuPont analysis, I always find it useful to do another couple of calculations to help me understand whether it is capital turnover or profit margins which is driving ROCE.

Using the data from Table 2.4, let's look at capital turnover first.

Capital turnover has improved from 1.042 (I am using the exact numbers here rather than rounded up ones so that you can clearly see what is going on) in 2013 to 1.234 in 2015. To see the effect on ROCE from the change in capital turnover only, you multiply the profit margin in 2013 by the 2015 capital turnover figure:

$$21.4\% \times 1.234 = 26.4\%$$

So the improvement in capital turnover alone has taken ROCE from 22.3% to 26.4%.

Turning to the effect from operating margins – to find this out we keep the capital turnover figure from 2013 of 1.042 unchanged and multiply it by the 2015 operating margin of 26.5%:

$$1.042 \times 26.5\% = 27.6\%$$

The change in operating margins alone has improved ROCE from 22.3% to 27.6%.

So we know that in this situation profit margins have had a bigger effect on ROCE than capital turnover, whilst the improvements in both ratios combined had a significant positive effect on Domino's ROCE.

Identifying the cause of profit margin improvements

It is very important to understand why a company's profit margins have changed, as was the case for Domino's between 2013 and 2015. You need to know whether these profit margins are sustainable in future years.

You can work this out by having a closer look at a company's sales and expenses. You can easily find the information you need in the notes to a company's annual accounts. The detail for Domino's is shown in Table 2.5.

We already know that there was a big increase in profits and profit margins from 2013 to 2015. By taking the 2013 numbers away from the 2015 numbers you can calculate the actual change. Domino's has added £47.9m of extra sales in that period (£316,788m – £268,902m), but costs have only increased by £22.6m (£243,607m – £220,986m). This means Domino's has converted over half its extra sales into profit.

Table 2.5: Domino's sales and operating costs

£000	2015	2014	2013	Change 2013–15
Sales	316,788	288,691	268,902	47,886
less:				
Cost of inventories (pizzas, etc.)	139,870	132,085	125,060	14,810
Depreciation & amortisation	6779	5824	5798	981
Operating leases	21,313	20,874	19,539	1774
Staff costs	39,288	34,851	32,042	7246
Other costs	36,357	32,726	38,547	-2190
Total costs	243,607	226,360	220,986	22,621
Operating profit	73,181	62,331	47,916	25,265
Margin	23.1%	21.6%	17.8%	52.8%

Looking at this another way, Domino's has turned a 17.8% increase in sales over two years (£47.9m increase from a base of £268.9m) into a 52.7% increase in profits (£25.3m increase from a base of £47.9m).

When profits increase much faster than sales this is an example of operational gearing. This is a good thing when sales are increasing, but the process also works in reverse and will decimate profits when sales fall.

Another thing you can do is look at how profit margins develop over time. You do this by expressing costs and profits as a percentage of sales. To do this, simply divide each number in the table above by the sales number. An example for Domino's is shown in Table 2.6. We start with sales being 100%.

Table 2.6: Domino's costs and profit as a percentage of sales

	2015	2014	2013
Sales	100.00%	100.00%	100.00%
less:			
Cost of inventories (pizzas etc)	44.15%	45.75%	46.51%
Depreciation & amortisation	2.14%	2.02%	2.16%
Operating leases	6.73%	7.23%	7.27%
Staff costs	12.40%	12.07%	11.92%
Other costs	11.48%	11.34%	14.33%
Total costs	76.90%	78.41%	82.18%
Operating profit	23.10%	21.59%	17.82%

We can see here that some costs have broadly stayed the same as a percentage of sales. However, the cost of inventories (for Domino's this is mainly pizza ingredients) has fallen by 2.36 percentage points and has been a driver of improved profit margins. 'Other costs' in the table have also fallen significantly from 14.3% of sales to 11.5% – this could reflect the increase in sales and possibly the mainly fixed nature of these other costs. That said, it can be very difficult for an outside investor to really know what is going on here.

Doing this kind of in-depth analysis for companies you are considering investing in will empower you with knowledge and understanding about a company which less diligent investors will miss.

The company report

Once you have completed an EBIT margin and DuPont analysis of a company and gained an impression of how that company is performing, you should read a company's annual report to see if it has anything to say about what you have found out.

In the case of Domino's in 2015, the findings of the analysis above are given a good explanation:

"Underlying operating profit increased by 16.6% to GBP73.2m, higher than system sales, demonstrating the favourable operational gearing from our operating model.

"During 2015, we and our franchisees enjoyed the benefits of a benign food price landscape with a record low cheese price, favourable wheat price and a fall in fuel costs. For the full year 2015 the average food basket in the UK saw a year-on-year decrease of 1.6% of store sales over 2014, which is a combination of the favourable food cost environment and the continued efforts of our supply chain procurement function to leverage the Group's buying power and secure the most competitive deals with quality suppliers. Food costs remain benign going into 2016."

As we can see, Domino's has confirmed the findings from our analysis that it has some operational gearing. This is good news as sales are currently rising. However, we have learned something significant here in that profits could fall sharply if sales fall and that operational gearing starts to work in reverse.

There is also a good explanation about profit margins. Operational gearing has helped profit margins to increase, but there has also been a benefit from lower ingredient costs such as cheese and wheat, as well as lower fuel costs. This is helpful now but prices can and do go up. If ingredient costs go up in the future, will Domino's profit margins go down?

One bit of reassuring news here is that the company says food costs are unlikely to rise in 2016, which should mean that profit margins can stay close to their current levels.

The company also mentions its improved buying power with suppliers. This is a benefit of getting bigger and makes the company a source of growth for its suppliers as well. This should allow it to get better prices from its suppliers, which can help margins and give it an edge over competitors

A good habit to learn when you are analysing any company is to do your own number crunching first before you read or listen to what the company has to say. By doing this, you build up your own picture of the company and its performance and then see if the company confirms your findings.

I always find this a very useful exercise as I have already learned a great deal before reading the company's comments. Those comments then enhance my understanding and can help give me an edge over less diligent investors who just rely on what the company says.

The other great benefit is that you learn to increasingly trust your own judgement and let the numbers describe the company you are looking at. Sometimes you will find that the company's comments about its own performance bear no resemblance to what has actually been going on. Management can often be overly optimistic or fail to address problems candidly. This is often a sign to stop researching a company, or to sell shares if you already own them.

The last two chapters have explained the importance of EBIT, profit margins, ROCE and DuPont analysis, and how they can help you identify good companies. Profits are very important but they need to be backed by another important hallmark of quality – cash flow. This is the subject of the next two chapters.

3

INTRODUCING FREE CASH FLOW

IN THIS CHAPTER, we look at arguably the most revealing item of financial information that a company gives investors: its cash flow statement.

The cash flow statement shows you where cash comes in and goes out of a company. If you want to really understand a company's finances and whether it might be a good investment then you need to look at its cash flow above everything else. By studying cash flow, you can identify quality companies and also learn how to spot the danger signs of companies that would make bad investments.

The bottom line for companies and investors is that cash matters. It is needed to pay bills, wages, interest on borrowings and dividends to shareholders. Investors can also use it to spot aggressive accounting by comparing profits with cash flows over a period of time. Time spent looking at a company's cash flows is therefore time spent usefully for the investor.

Specifically, this chapter introduces the topic of free cash flow, why it is so important and how quality companies generate free cash flow. Then, in Chapter 4, I move on to look at how you can use free cash flow numbers to identify good companies to invest in and bad ones to stay away from.

An example cash flow statement from Domino's is shown in Table 3.1.

Table 3.1: Domino's cash flow statement

£m unless stated	2010	2011	2012	2013	2014	2015
Cash flows						
Operating profit	35.4	39.0	41.7	18.0	61.3	71.5

£m unless stated	2010	2011	2012	2013	2014	2015
Depreciation & amortisation	2.8	3.3	4.7	5.8	5.8	6.8
Profit on disposals	-	-	[0.5]	[1.9]	[1.1]	0.08
Change in stock	[2.3]	1.2	[3.3]	3.1	[0.6]	[1.4]
Change in debtors	[3.7]	[9.9]	[6]	1.7	[1.6]	1.8
Change in creditors	7.3	[1.4]	12.3	[3.5]	11.1	5.9
Change in provisions	0.07	1.8	1.5	21.6	[0.06]	4.4
Change in working capital	1.4	[8.3]	4.5	22.9	8.8	10.7
Other (operating)	1.4	1.5	3.6	4.4	[6.3]	[8.7]
Operating cash flow	41	35.5	54.1	49.3	68.5	80.4
Tax paid	[5.5]	[4]	[6.6]	[8.6]	[8.1]	[11.4]
Net cash from operations	35.6	31.5	47.5	40.7	60.4	69.0
Capital expenditure	[11.6]	[13]	[4.4]	[8.1]	[4.4]	[6.8]
Sale of fixed assets	0.06	0.6	-	-	-	-
Acquisitions	-	-	[8.3]	-	-	-
Sale of businesses	-	0.03	0.8	2.4	-	-
Interest received	-	-	-	-	-	-
Other investments received	-	-	-	-	-	-
Dividends from joint ventures	0.02	0.07	0.07	0.06	0.04	0.5
Other (investing)	1.0	[4.6]	[18.5]	1.5	1.6	[4.7]
Net cash from investing	[10.5]	[16.9]	[30.3]	[4.2]	[2.8]	[11.0]
New share issues	1.6	0.6	2.6	2.2	2.0	3.6
Share buyback	[4.7]	[2.2]	[3.3]	-	[2.2]	-
New borrowing	1.6	1.3	6.5	-	31.9	5.7
Repayment of borrowing	[2.5]	[2.2]	[2.8]	[4.2]	[56.3]	[16.3]
Equity dividends paid	[13.6]	[18]	[21.7]	[24.6]	[27.5]	[31.0]
Dividends paid to minorities	-	-	-	-	-	-
Interest paid	[0.02]	[0.5]	[0.7]	[0.9]	[0.08]	[0.3]
Other (financing)	-	-	[0.0]	0.1	[2.9]	[0.008]
Net cash from financing	[17.8]	[21.1]	[19.5]	[27.3]	[55.7]	[38.4]
Net change in cash	**7.2**	**[6.5]**	**[2.3]**	**9.2**	**1.9**	**19.6**

Below, I begin by explaining why cash flow isn't simply the same as profit and then move on to look at free cash flow.

Why profits and cash flow are not the same number

Cash flow is the lifeblood of any business. There have been numerous companies that seemed to be very profitable, but were teetering on the edge of bankruptcy because they couldn't turn their profits into cash fast enough.

A very high profile example of this in recent years is software company Globo. This company seemed to be very profitable and growing rapidly, but it wasn't turning its profits into enough cash, as shown in Table 3.2.

Table 3.2: Globo's free cash flow (fcf) and post-tax profits (2006–2014)

Globo £000s	Post-tax profit	Free cash flow	Difference	Difference (%)
2007	2002	−3839	−5841	−292%
2008	2380	−4683	−7063	−297%
2009	2828	-965	−3793	−134%
2010	4391	−5416	−9807	−223%
2011	8880	−9347	−18,227	−205%
2012	17,804	1688	−16,116	−91%
2013	25,332	5240	−20,092	−79%
2014	35,011	7319	−27,692	−79%

Source: Annual accounts

In Table 3.2 you can see that post-tax profits were rising over this period, but free cash flow was not. It turned out that Globo's profits were largely illusory and it filed for bankruptcy in 2015.

It is important to understand that profits and cash flow are not the same thing, and it is not sufficient for a company to be profitable to make it a good investment.

Profits are calculated on the basis of something known as accruals, or matching. This means that a company's revenues and the costs of generating them are matched against each other and recorded when a transaction takes place. This does not tell you when cash came in or went out of the business – the flow of cash, or cash flow. The cash flow is generally received or paid at different times to the date of a transaction or delivery. For example, a customer can pay in advance or a bill can be paid after 30 days.

This means that profits will never be exactly the same as its cash flow. There are lots of reasons why this is the case, but I'll give you three quick examples now:

1. *Depreciation*: This is an expense in the annual income statement which matches the cost of a tangible fixed asset against the revenues it produces. It reduces the amount of profit a company makes in a year. However, it is not a cash flow. The actual cash flow happened when the company bought the asset that is being depreciated, which could have been years ago.

2. *Sales on credit*: Customers are often given a period of time to pay for the goods and services they buy from a company. This sale will usually be booked in the income statement before the cash is received.

3. *Purchases on credit*: Companies may buy supplies on credit. These will sometimes be expensed in the income statement before the bill has been paid. Also, companies can pay for supplies in advance (a prepayment), which means that cash has flowed out of the company before the costs of supplies has been expensed in the income statement.

And so what the investor needs to do, after finding out that a company is profitable, is to see how good that company is at turning its profits into cash flow.

Let's look at why investors should care a great deal about cash flow, before moving on to look at an example of how to work out a company's cash flow.

The importance of free cash flow for investors

Good companies produce lots of *free cash flow*. Free cash flow is the amount of money left over after a company has paid for things that it cannot avoid. Such as:

- The interest on any debts.

- Its tax bill.

- Keeping its assets in good working order so it can continue providing goods and services for customers, or purchasing new assets to help the company carry out or grow its business. This is called capital expenditure (capex).

Once a company has paid its debts and bills, and invested in any necessary capex, it is free to do anything it wants with its remaining cash: this is its free cash flow. For example, it can use the cash to:

- Pay dividends to shareholders.

- Buy back its own shares.

- Repay debt.

- Buy other companies.

All of these things have the potential to give a company's shareholders a healthy return on their investment.

This is why I say that a company's future free cash flow is the ultimate determinant of how good an investment the company will be. As I will show later in the book, cash flow is the key determinant of its share price and the size of the dividends it will pay out to shareholders – which are the two elements that comprise the total returns from owning a share.

After all this talk about the importance of cash flow, it is now time to look at how to calculate it.

How to calculate free cash flow

There are two main definitions of free cash flow, both of which are useful for investors:

1. Free cash flow to the firm.
2. Free cash flow for shareholders (also referred to as free cash flow for equity).

You can calculate both of these very easily from a company's cash flow statement.

To calculate free cash flow to the firm (FCFF), take a company's cash flows from operating activities, add dividends received from joint ventures and subtract tax paid to get the net cash flow from operations. Then subtract capex.

To get the free cash flow for shareholders (FCF), take the FCFF number and subtract net interest (interest received less interest paid), any preference share dividends, and dividends to minority shareholders.

As with previous chapters, I have chosen to use Domino's Pizza as an example to show you how to use cash flow information.

The calculation for Domino's is shown in Table 3.3 and a chart showing the ten-year record of FCFF and FCF is provided in Figure 3.1.

For example, in 2015 Domino's had net cash from operations of £69m. To calculate FCFF we deduct capex of £6.8m and add dividends from joint ventures of £0.5m. This gives a result of £62.7m.

To calculate FCF, we take this figure of £62.7m and subtract net interest received of £0.1m, which gives £62.6m. You can see all of these figures in Table 3.3.

Table 3.3: Free cash flow calculations for Domino's

£m unless stated	2010	2011	2012	2013	2014	2015
Free cash flow						
Net cash from operations	35.6	31.5	47.5	40.7	60.4	69.0
Capital expenditure	[11.6]	[13.0]	[4.4]	[8.1]	[4.4]	6.8
Dividends from joint ventures	0.02	0.07	0.07	0.06	0.04	0.5
Free cash flow for firm (FCFF)	24.0	18.5	43.1	32.6	56.0	62.7
Dividends paid to minorities	[13.6]	-	-	-	-	-
Interest paid	[0.2]	[0.5]	[0.7]	[0.9]	[0.8]	[0.3]
Interest received	0.2	0.2	0.2	0.2	0.2	0.2
Free cash flow for equity (FCF)	10.4	18.2	42.6	31.9	55.4	62.6

Despite a slight blip in 2013, Domino's was able to grow its net cash from operations and free cash flow to the firm over the period 2006 to 2015. The free cash flow for its shareholders followed suit.

You can see that Domino's has very little debt and a tiny interest payment, which means virtually all of the free cash flow produced by the business (FCFF) becomes free cash for the shareholders (FCF). In other words, there is not much difference between FCFF and FCF for Domino's. This is a positive sign for investors and you should look for this sort of situation in companies you are analysing.

As a contrast to that situation at Domino's, let's take a look at pub and brewing company Greene King, where the FCFF and FCF have been consistently different over the last ten years (see Figure 3.2). Greene King is able to generate a decent and consistent level of FCFF, but it has lots of borrowings and therefore interest bills to pay. The interest payments have been eating up a big chunk of the company's FCFF, leaving less FCF for shareholders.

In general, it is a good idea to avoid companies with lots of debt. Too much of their free cash flow to the firm can end up being paid in interest to lenders instead of to shareholders.

The one possible exception to this rule is when companies are using their free cash flows to repay debt and lower their future interest bills. This can see FCF to shareholders increasing significantly in the future, which can sometimes make the shares of companies repaying debt good ones to own.

We have seen that Domino's has a very good long-term track record of producing free cash flow for its shareholders. But how is a company able to do this?

Figure 3.1: Domino's FCFF and FCF, 2006–2015

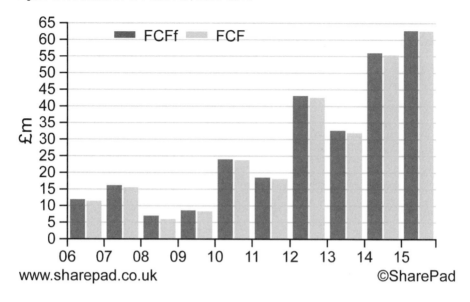

Figure 3.2: Greene King FCFF and FCF, 2006–2015

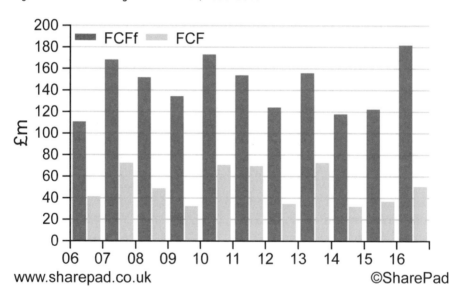

How companies produce lots of free cash flow

Companies that produce lots of free cash flow can make excellent investments. By looking at how a company produces free cash flow you can understand why:

1. The company is very profitable, with growing profits, and those growing profits are converted into a growing amount of operating cash flow (this is operating cash conversion).

2. The company only needs to spend small amounts of money on new assets – capex – to grow its profits (the company has low capex requirements).

Let's look at each of these points in turn.

1. Operating cash conversion

Quality companies turn their operating profits into free cash flow. As ever, the best way for me to explain how an investor should investigate this is through a real company example.

We already know from the previous chapter that Domino's is a very profitable business. Let's see how good it has been at turning its operating profits (EBIT) into cash. The way to measure this is with the *operating cash conversion ratio*, which is defined as:

operating cash conversion ratio = (operating cash flow/operating profit) x 100%

This ratio gives the investor an insight into the quality or otherwise of a company's profits. Ideally, we want to see a company consistently turning all its operating profits into operating cash flow. This will be reflected by an operating cash conversion ratio of 100% or above. Not only does this make a company's profits more believable but also it means that it will have a stronger financial position – and less need to borrow money – than a company that has to wait for some of its profits to turn into cash.

The operating cash conversion ratio for Domino's over the last ten years is shown in Figure 3.3. With the exception of 2011, Domino's has consistently achieved a ratio of 100% over the last ten years.

As you can see, the two components needed to calculate the operating cash conversion ratio are the operating profit and the operating cash flow. Table 3.4 shows the data for calculating the operating cash flow from the operating profit for 2010 to 2015.

Figure 3.3: Domino's operating cash conversion ratio, 2005–2016

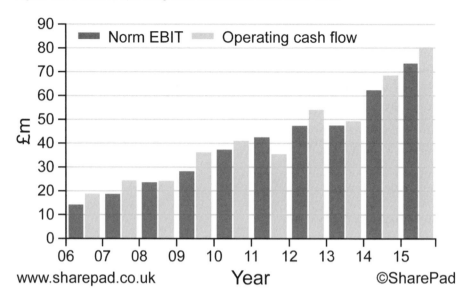

www.sharepad.co.uk Year ©SharePad

Table 3.4: Domino's operating profit and operating cash flow, 2010–2015

£m unless stated	2010	2011	2012	2013	2014	2015
Operating profit	35.7	39.4	42.7	20.4	62.3	73.2
Depreciation & amortisation	2.8	3.3	4.7	5.8	5.8	6.8
Profit on disposals	-	-	[0.5]	[1.9]	[1.1]	0.08
Change in stock	[2.3]	1.2	[3.3]	3.1	[0.6]	[1.4]
Change in debtors	[3.7]	[9.9]	[6]	1.7	[1.6]	1.8
Change in creditors	7.3	[1.4]	12.3	[3.5]	11.1	5.9
Change in provisions	0.07	1.8	1.5	21.6	[0.06]	4.4
Change in working capital	1.3	[10.1]	2.5	[0.5	7.7	6.4
Other (operating)	1.3	2.9	4.7	25.5	[6.2]	[6.1]
Operating cash flow	41	35.5	54.1	49.3	68.5	80.4
Tax paid	[5.5]	[4]	[6.6]	[8.8]	[8.1]	[11.4]
Net cash from operations	35.6	31.5	47.5	40.7	60.4	69

When we convert from operating profit to operating cash flow, what happens is that any expense – such as depreciation – which reduced operating profit but did not see cash flow out of the business is added to the operating profit. Any income that did not cause cash to come into the business is taken away from operating profit.

Let's look at how Domino's 2015 operating profit of £73.2m was converted into operating cash flow.

The main adjustments that you are likely to come across when calculating the operating cash flow number are:

- *Depreciation & amortisation*: **add back**. In 2015, £6.8m has reduced operating profits but, as it was not a cash flow, it is added back to operating cash flow.

- *Profit/losses on disposals*: **take away/add back**. A profit or loss on the sale (disposal) of an asset compared to the asset's value on the balance sheet (or book value). This is included in operating profit but the cash received from the sale is included in the investing section of the cash flow statement. The profit or loss (the difference between the cash received and the asset value on the balance sheet) is used to adjust the company's operating cash flow. A loss is added back to operating profit and a profit is taken away. In 2015, Domino's made a small loss of £0.08m which very slightly increased operating cash flow.

- *Increases/decreases in debtors (sales made on credit)*: **take away/add back**. If a company makes a sale on credit it creates a debtor and has to wait for the cash from the sale to be paid. During the year it will also receive cash from sales from the previous year made on credit. If a company is growing its sales then often its outstanding debtors will grow as well. If debtors grow faster than sales then the company is giving more credit to its customers – not ideal. If debtors goes down compared to sales then the company is tightening its credit – perhaps by chasing debtors harder. In 2015, Domino's debtor balance fell by £1.8m, in spite of an increase of sales – which is impressive. This increases operating cash flow but does not affect operating profit.

- *Increases/decreases in creditors (purchases made on credit)*: **add back/take away.** Companies can make purchases on credit. This means they don't have to pay for goods or services straightaway. This increases their trade creditors balance. The balance will decrease as payments are made. An increase in this balance means that the company gets a temporary cash benefit to operating cash flow. If the balance reduces – if suppliers want paying faster – cash flows out of the company which reduces operating cash flow. Domino's gained a £5.9m cash flow benefit from creditors in 2015, which increases operating cash flow.

- *Increases/decreases in stock levels (inventory)*: **take away/add back**. Companies will make or buy in stock of raw materials or goods to sell to their customers. Building up stocks requires cash to be spent. If more stock is added than is sold, a company's stock or inventory balances will increase and this will show as a cash flow out of the company and reduced operating cash flow. It will not affect operating profit. If a company is selling its stocks faster than it is buying raw material, this balance will decrease and the change will be shown as a cash flow added back to operating profit. Operating with inventory levels that are too low can generate expensive problems (such as no pizza to sell if there is a sudden dramatic increase in demand). In general expect stock levels to go up and down with sales levels. Domino's stock balance increased by £1.4m in 2015, which reduces operating cash flow.

- *Amount paid into a final salary pension fund is more/less than pension cost expensed in the income statement*: **take away/add back**. When calculating operating profit, the expense for an employee's final salary pension scheme is based on a regular contribution made by the company in respect to the amount of pension benefits earned by employees during the year (e.g. 1/60th of their expected final salary). In recent years, final salary pension schemes have become problematic for some companies as the money in the pension fund has not been enough to pay the promised pensions in the future. This has meant that cash top up payments in excess of the regular expense have been required. This is shown by a reduction in a company's operating cash flow and is a deduction from the starting operating profit figure. Domino's does not have a final salary pension scheme so this is not an issue. I will have more to say on pension funds later in the book.

These items above added together make up the annual change in a company's working capital. Working capital refers to the amount of cash a company needs to undertake its day-to-day activities. If working capital is increasing, then this shows the amount of cash a company might need to borrow – from a bank overdraft facility – to finance its day-to-day activities as it waits for cash to flow in. The smaller a company's working capital requirement, the better its cash flow and financial position tends to be.

That's a fairly long list and quite a lot to take in, but hopefully after you've looked at a few cash flow statements you will be able to understand how a company is, or isn't, generating its cash.

We can see for Domino's in 2015 that £73.2m of operating profit was turned into £80.4m of operating cash flow once all the adjustments had taken place. That is an operating cash conversion ratio of 109.8%.

Interpreting the operating cash conversion ratio

I have said that turning operating profit into operating cash flow is a desirable characteristic of companies. It is. But that doesn't mean that an operating cash conversion ratio of more than 100% is a sign that you have found a great business.

It's not as simple as this. It doesn't mean that a company will go on to produce lots of free cash flow.

For example, companies that have lots of fixed assets, such as manufacturers, hotels, oil explorers, miners or utility networks, will tend to have very big depreciation expenses, which boost their operating cash flow when these expenses are added back to operating profit. This will tend to give these sorts of companies a high operating cash conversion ratio, as shown in Table 3.5. You can spot such companies by looking at the ratio between depreciation and operating cash flow, which is shown in the second column from the right in Table 3.5.

Table 3.5: Companies with high depreciation to operating cash flow (**2015/16**)

	Depreciation & amortisation (£m)	Operating cash flow (£m)	Depreciation & amortisation as % of operating cash flow (%)	Operating cash conversion (%)
Sainsbury (J)	584	624	93.6%	118.9%
Vodafone Group	9498	11220	84.7%	549.7%
Royal Dutch Shell	17,396	24,408	71.3%	652.3%
FirstGroup	378	533	70.8%	215.0%
BHP Billiton	5846	8553	68.4%	113.9%
BT Group	2630	5435	48.4%	143.7%
United Utilities Group	364	906	40.2%	118.3%

Source: SharePad

Whilst a high operating cash conversion ratio is welcome and is better than having a ratio of less than 100%, you will also tend to see that big depreciation expenses mean big capex bills and the cash generated from depreciation has to be ploughed back into the business to keep those assets in good condition. This means the cash doesn't tend to end up flowing to shareholders.

When you come across a company with high levels of operating cash conversion, always calculate the depreciation and amortisation expenses as a percentage of operating cash flow as well. As a rule of thumb, avoid companies with a depreciation to operating cash flow ratio of more than 30%, because this tends to mean that at least 30% of operating cash flow will have to be spent maintaining assets.

As I will explain shortly, good companies are ones that don't need to spend a lot of money to grow. So when it comes to operating cash conversion, you are better off looking for high conversion rates with low depreciation to operating cash flow ratios. Table 3.6 gives examples of some companies that meet that criteria.

Table 3.6: Companies with low depreciation to operating cash flow (2015/16)

	Depreciation & amortisation (£m)	Operating cash flow (£m)	Depreciation & amortisation % of operating cash flow (%)	Operating cash conversion (%)
Rightmove	1	143	0.9	104.4
British American Tobacco	404	5400	7.5	109.4
Domino's Pizza UK & IRL	7	80	8.2	111.6
Diageo	355	3360	10.6	120.4
Sage Group (The)	47	419	11.3	116.5
InterContinental Hotels	63	528	11.9	122.5
Dignity	15	122	12.0	127.7

The other thing you need to keep an eye on when looking at operating cash conversion is the amount of cash flowing out of a business due to changes in working capital – stocks, debtors and creditors. High levels can be a sign of financial distress or aggressive accounting.

With stocks (or inventory), a rising balance sees cash flowing out of the company. This is usually fine if the company is building them up in anticipation of extra sales, but if it becomes a trend or is not due to higher anticipated future sales it could be a sign of trouble. If a company has too many stocks then it might have to reduce its selling prices to get rid of them, which will reduce future profits.

If you come across a company with regular cash outflows from increases in stocks, compare the stock or inventory figure on the company's balance sheet with its turnover or revenue figure on the income statement as a percentage. This will give you its stock or inventory ratio:

stock ratio = stock/turnover × 100%

A rising stock ratio can be a sign of company weakness. Domino's had a closing stock balance of £6.2m in 2015 compared with turnover of £316.8m, giving it a stock ratio of 1.95%. This is a very low number and not materially different from previous years, as shown in Figure 3.4.

Stock levels are particularly relevant for manufacturing and retailing companies and need to be watched closely.

Figure 3.4: Domino's stock and work in progress (WIP) ratio (2006–2015)

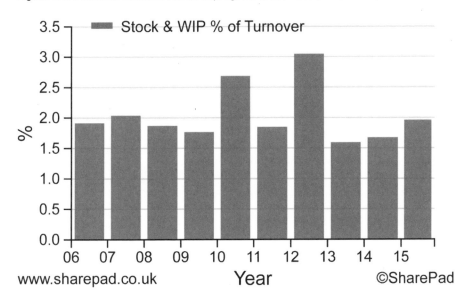

www.sharepad.co.uk   **Year**   ©SharePad

If you are looking for signs of aggressive accounting, then the debtors number in the cash flow statement is something you should be keeping an eye on. A company can grow its turnover quickly by giving customers generous credit terms. This means that a sale can be booked in the income statement but the company will have to wait longer to be paid. Sometimes, the cash is never received.

A cash outflow from debtors is not necessarily a problem and is expected from a company that is growing. But if this is accompanied by a rise in the debtor ratio then it can be a sign that something is amiss. The debtor ratio can be calculated as follows:

debtor ratio = trade debtors/turnover × 100%.

Domino's only had £8m of trade debtors at the end of 2015 giving it a very small debtor ratio of 2.5%, as shown in Figure 3.5.

However, Redcentric, a software company listed on the Alternative Investment Market (AIM), saw its share price crash in November 2016 due to it revealing that it had misstated its profits. A close look at its operating cash flow would have shown a big outflow of cash from debtors in 2016 and a big increase in the debtor ratio (see Figure 3.6) – a warning sign that should have been heeded.

Figure 3.5: Domino's debtor ratio (2005–2015)

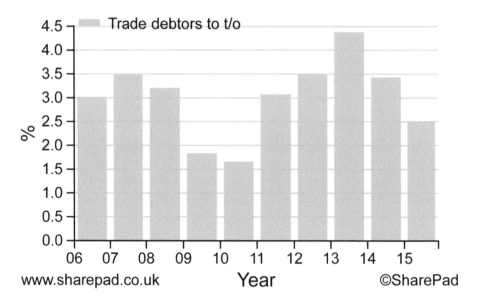

www.sharepad.co.uk   ©SharePad

Figure 3.6: Redcentric debtor ratio (2014–2016)

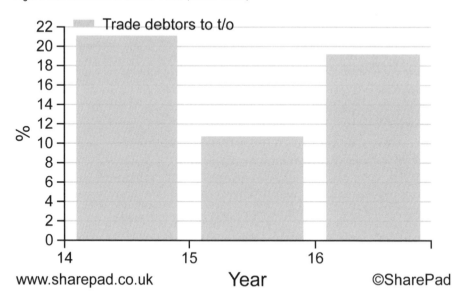

www.sharepad.co.uk   ©SharePad

When it comes to cash outflows from changes in creditors, you need to be wary of very big changes. This is telling you that a company's suppliers are demanding faster payment. This could be a sign of a loss of buying power, a weakness in the financial position of the company, or even imminent bankruptcy.

To sum up, high quality companies convert their operating profits into operating cash flow. They do it without having large depreciation expenses or big cash outflows from working capital. This is the first step to a company producing lots of free cash flow.

The second and most important step is a company having low capex requirements.

2. Low capex requirements

Quality companies produce high ROCE (at least 15%) and lots of free cash flow because they don't need to spend much money on new assets in order to grow. One way you can spot whether a company fits this pattern is to calculate its capex ratio. The capex ratio is defined as:

capex ratio = capex/operating cash flow

This ratio compares the amount of cash a company ploughs back into its business through capex to the amount of cash coming into the business – its operating cash flow. The lower this ratio, the less capital intensive a company is and the better chance it has of producing lots of free cash flow and a high ROCE. I usually look for a capex ratio of lower than 30%.

It is very easy to calculate a capex ratio for a company. Go to its cash flow statement and find the line labelled 'capital expenditure' or 'purchase of fixed assets'. Then divide that number by the operating cash flow number.

Domino's capex ratio in 2015 was £6.8m/£80.4m = 8.45%.

Table 3.7 shows a list of non-financial companies in the FTSE 350 index in November 2016 with the lowest capex ratios. You can see that they also have very high ROCE figures as well.

Table 3.7: FTSE 350 companies with low capex ratios (November 2016)

Name	Capex ratio (%)	ROCE (%)
Rightmove	1.2	929.9
Auto Trader Group	1.7	45.0
Zoopla Property Group	1.7	22.8
Softcat	4.6	48.5
Sage Group (The)	5.4	23.0

Name	Capex ratio (%)	ROCE (%)
Indivior	6.3	98.4
Diploma	6.9	27.5
Euromoney Institutional Investor	7.5	26.8
ITV	8.0	40.2
Domino's Pizza UK & IRL	8.4	32.7
Hays	10.4	24.2
British American Tobacco	11.1	20.3
PayPoint	11.9	49.6
PageGroup	14.9	24.2
Spirax-Sarco Engineering	19.0	23.0
Next	19.4	33.2
AA	19.6	23.6
Paddy Power Betfair	19.7	33.8
Moneysupermarket.com Group	20.0	43.8
QinetiQ Group	22.6	28.4
Dunelm Group	22.9	22.7
Howden Joinery Group	23.7	28.6
InterContinental Hotels Group	24.6	26.9

Companies with high capex ratios tend to have a very low ROCE. A selection of high capex ratio companies is shown in Table 3.8.

Table 3.8: FTSE 350 companies with high capex ratios (November 2016)

Name	Capex ratio (%)	ROCE (%)
Tullow Oil	160.5	2.2
Antofagasta	131.2	2.3
Acacia Mining	117.7	3.3
Drax Group	109.1	7.9
Sainsbury (J)	109.0	6.8
Ocado Group	107.1	5.9
Vodafone Group	105.7	2.4
Anglo American	100.3	3.4

Name	Capex ratio (%)	ROCE (%)
Regus	84.0	8.9
Travis Perkins	83.5	9.2
Fresnillo	82.2	5.8
Marston's	79.7	8.6
SSE	79.6	9.1
SIG	79.5	7.8
Rolls-Royce Group	79.0	9.8
Greencore Group	78.6	9.1
United Utilities Group	77.3	6.5
Pennon Group	76.4	5.1
FirstGroup	76.0	5.6

Generally speaking, I find that companies with capex ratios of 30% or more tend not to produce very high ROCE. That's why, ideally, I tend to look for companies where the capex ratio is consistently below 30%.

Figure 3.7 shows the capex ratio for Domino's for 2006 to 2015.

Figure 3.7: Domino's capex ratio, 2006–2015

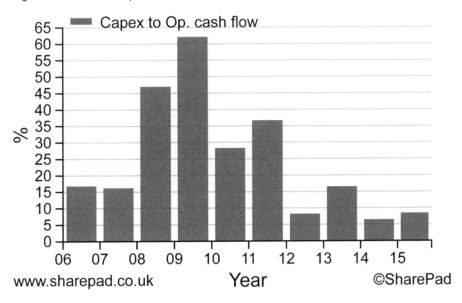

The chart shows that Domino's capex ratio has declined significantly in recent years and is now less than 10% of operating cash flow. Previously it was much higher, as in 2008 and 2009 the company was investing in new distribution centres to help grow the business.

Investors need to ask whether the company can keep on growing without having to open more distribution centres in the future. If it can, then the capex ratio should remain low and the company's free cash flow prospects will continue to be favourable.

A high capex ratio is sometimes necessary in order to give a company the scope to grow. This is not usually a problem, as capex will tend to fall back afterwards (as in the case of Domino's in Figure 3.7). However, when the capex ratio is consistently high year after year this is a warning sign for investors.

For an example of a company that has had a high capex ratio for the last ten years, let's look at Royal Dutch Shell. Its capex ratio for 2006 to 2015 is shown in Figure 3.8. As you can see, Shell consistently ploughed more than half its operating cash flow back into its business with capex in this period.

Figure 3.8: Royal Dutch Shell's capex ratio (2005–2016)

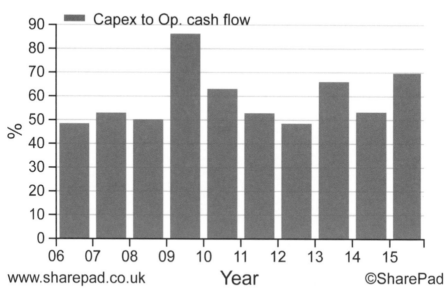

This consistently high capex ratio – along with volatile oil prices – meant that Shell's free cash flow moved around all over the place in this period, before plunging in 2015. This is illustrated in Figure 3.9.

Figure 3.9: Royal Dutch Shell's FCFF (2005–2016)

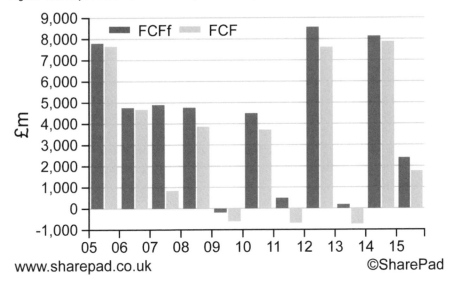

www.sharepad.co.uk ©SharePad

Given what you now know about the importance of free cash flow in quality companies, you should not be surprised to learn that in the ten years to June 2016, Domino's trounced Shell as an investment. Domino's returned nearly 660%, compared with just 63% for Shell. The divergent share price performance of the two companies is illustrated in Figure 3.10.

Figure 3.10: Share price performance of Domino's, Royal Dutch Shell (2005–2016)

*   *   *

This chapter has shown what quality companies do to produce lots of free cash flow. In the next chapter, I'll show you how you can use free cash flow to further enhance your understanding of a company and to pick great shares to own.

4

ADVANCED FREE CASH FLOW ANALYSIS

IN THE PREVIOUS chapter we looked at how companies can produce lots of free cash flow. In this chapter, I show you how to take free cash flow analysis of a company on to the next level.

We are going to get behind those free cash flow numbers so that you can use them to identify quality companies. You'll learn what to look out for when examining a company's free cash flow that will allow you to spot the differences between good and bad businesses.

The specific topics are:

1. Is a company spending enough?

2. Is negative cash flow always bad?

3. Combining ROCE and free cash flow.

4. Free cash flow per share.

5. How safe are dividend payments?

6. When free cash flow is not what it seems.

7. Manipulation of free cash flow.

We now look at each of these topics in turn.

1. How do you know if a company is spending enough?

A business which doesn't need to spend a lot of money to grow is always preferable to one that does. However, sometimes a company can spend too little on its assets. If its capex spend is too low, the condition of its assets can deteriorate, which can blunt a company's competitive edge. Its free cash flow may not be sustainable because it will need to eventually spend a lot of money replacing worn-out assets.

As an outsider you can never be completely sure if a company is spending enough to maintain its existing assets – known as its *maintenance* or *stay in business* capex. What investors can do is check to see if a company is spending more on capex than its depreciation and amortisation expenses. If it is, then that can often be a sign that a company is spending enough.

NOTE: You will see reference to depreciation and amortisation in company accounts and in this book. Amortisation is the equivalent of depreciation, but for intangible assets such as software or licences.

I'll show you how to estimate how much a company needs to spend on maintenance capex in Part 3. For now, let's return to our familiar example of Domino's to check on its capex.

Figure 4.1 shows that Domino's capex has consistently been the same as or more than its depreciation charge in the period 2006 to 2015. Where you see a situation like this, this is an encouraging sign for the investor.

It is also a good idea to compare capex to depreciation ratios with similar companies in the same line of business, to see if a company is spending more or less than the industry average. Domino's is in the FTSE 350 Restaurants and Bars Sector. You can find similar companies by looking in the financial sections of newspapers where the share prices are listed.

You should compare the capex to depreciation ratio with other companies for the last year. It's also a good idea to look at the average over a period of five years or more, as a single year's capex might not be representative of normal spending. An analysis for Domino's and similar companies is shown in Table 4.1.

Here we can see that Domino's is at the lower end of the sector in terms of capex spending. If you come across a company that is spending less than depreciation – such as JD Wetherspoon – you need to check if that is really the case. Closer inspection of its accounts reveals that it only classifies maintenance capex as capex, with spending on new pubs covered elsewhere in the cash flow statement.

Figure 4.1: Domino's capex and depreciation & amortisation (2006–2015)

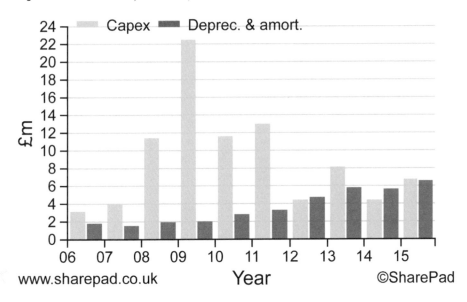

Year

Table 4.1: Capex to depreciation over one year and five years for Domino's and similar companies

Name	Capex (£m)	Depreciation & amortisation (£m)	Capex to depreciation (%)	Capex to depreciation 5y avg (%)
Compass Group	504	366	137.7	443.4
Domino's Pizza UK & IRL	7	7	102.7	162.5
Greene King	194	105	185.4	229.0
Marston's	142	38	375.5	373.8
Mitchells & Butlers	160	111	144.1	135.0
Restaurant Group (The)	75	39	191.3	190.2
SSP Group	82	78	104.7	95.4
Wetherspoon (JD)	34	72	46.4	79.1
Whitbread	716	188	381.8	291

Sometimes you will come across a company where capex spending is considerably below the depreciation and amortisation expense on a regular basis and it will not be a problem. ITV plc is a good example of this (see Figure 4.2).

Figure 4.2: ITV capex and depreciation & amortisation (2006–2015)

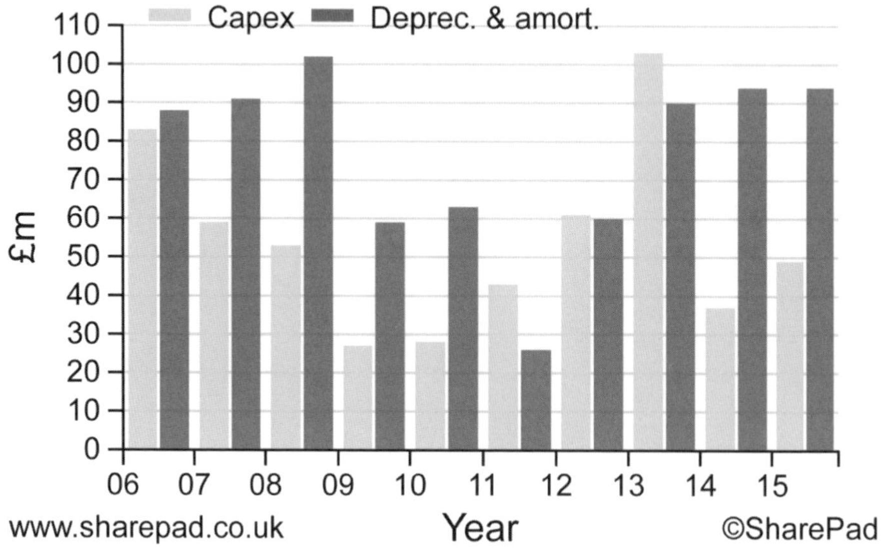

Does this mean that ITV is under-investing and has unsustainable free cash flow?

As you can see from the chart, this is not a new situation for ITV and the pattern has been the same over a period of years. This is due to the nature of the business that ITV is in: it has to spread the cost of things such as licences, customer contracts, software and programme libraries over their useful lives and these do not need to be matched by outflows of cash every year. In my view, there is nothing worrying going on here from the investor's point of view.

This is a reminder that is not sufficient for an investor to look at a company's financial numbers in isolation; you always need to think about what type of company this is, and consider its specific circumstances to help you make sense of what the numbers are showing.

What an investor should watch out for is companies which cut capex to save cash in times of difficulty, such as when the company is faced with falling revenues and falling profits. Sooner or later, it will have to replace worn-out assets and this will likely see free cash flow fall.

As ever, the ideal situation is a company that has stable or growing revenues and profits, and stable capex against depreciation and amortisation, over a period of years.

2. Is negative free cash flow always bad?

In my opinion, the best companies to buy are ones that have large and growing amounts of free cash flow. One possible drawback of this approach is that you will ignore companies with small or even negative free cash flows because they are investing heavily in new assets to grow their future sales, profits and operating cash flows.

Should you really ignore companies like this?

Not necessarily. Ideally you will try to find companies that don't need to spend a lot of capex to grow. However, if you come across what appears to be a quality company that is spending a lot of money, then you need to make sure the company is getting a good return on that investment.

You need to look at the trend in ROCE at the same time as you are looking at free cash flow. If ROCE is high and rising whilst a company is spending heavily then the company could start generating lots of free cash flow when its spending settles down – if it ever does.

The main issue is how much money the company needs to spend to maintain its assets in a steady state. As I mentioned earlier, I'll have more to say on this topic in Part 3 of the book when I discuss how to value companies.

The point here is that you might be making a mistake by ignoring companies with low or negative free cash flow. There could be a great cash flow business waiting to blossom.

Let's look at a couple of examples of companies that have invested heavily in future growth.

easyJet – investing heavily in assets

One company that has spent a lot on new assets in recent years is easyJet. Its capex-to-depreciation ratio was well over 100% for the period 2006 to 2015, which shows that it has been investing heavily in its assets. This is illustrated in Figure 4.3.

Owing to this heavy investment, easyJet's free cash flow performance over the same ten-year period between 2006 and 2016 had been patchy, with many years of negative free cash flow. This is shown in Figure 4.4.

Figure 4.3: easyJet capex to depreciation & amortisation ratio and ROCE (2006–2015)

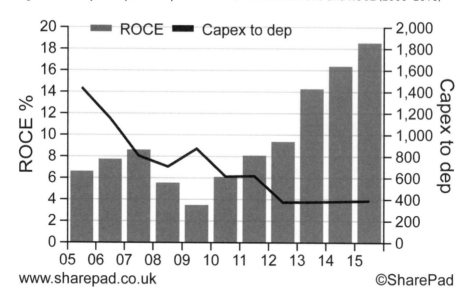

Figure 4.4: easyJet FCFF (2006–2015)

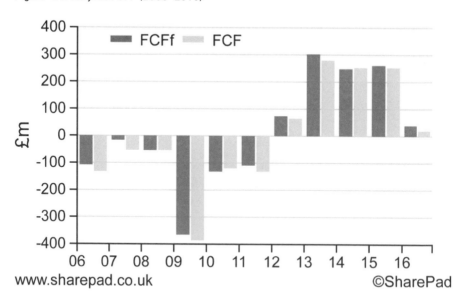

These free cash flow levels are not encouraging for the investor, but if you look again at Figure 4.3 you can see that ROCE was on an encouraging upward trend in this period.

ROCE improved significantly to reach a very respectable 18%, and this helped free cash flow to grow as well. Yet, in 2015, capex to depreciation was still 400%. If easyJet was to stop investing aggressively and cut its capex as a percentage of depreciation, whilst maintaining its ROCE on existing assets, its free cash flow could grow significantly. This would make its shares a more obviously attractive investment.

It must be noted that the high levels of investment could pay off in future years.

In summary, keep an eye on companies that have a high capex to depreciation ratio, and a growing ROCE. These companies could generate cash flows for investors in the future if ROCE is maintained.

Sainsbury's – variable free cash flows and disappointing ROCE

A different sort of situation can be seen at Sainsbury's, for which Figure 4.5 shows that free cash flow has been up and down a lot over the period from 2006 to 2015.

Figure 4.5: Sainsbury's FCFF (2006–2015)

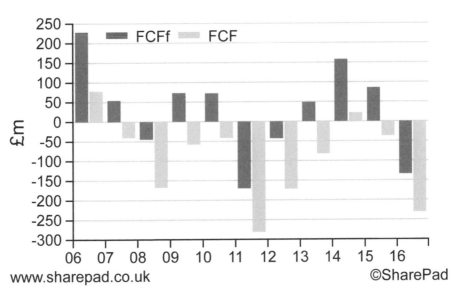

www.sharepad.co.uk   ©SharePad

The problem for Sainsbury's is that its profits have been falling but capex has still been higher than depreciation. Despite growing its asset base, ROCE has been very disappointing, as shown in Figure 4.6.

Figure 4.6: Sainsbury's capex to depreciation & amortisation ratio and ROCE (2006–2015)

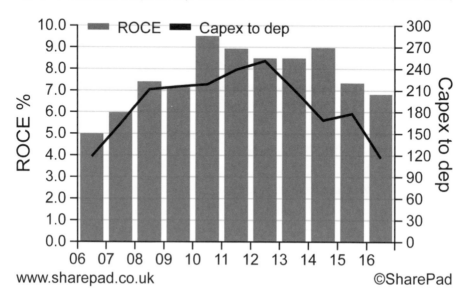

The message here is that Sainsbury's does not look as if it will be in a position to generate excess free cash flows for investors any time soon. From our point of view, it does not appear to represent a good investment.

3. Combining ROCE and free cash flow: CROCI

In Chapter 2, I identified great companies as ones that could consistently produce a high ROCE. In Chapter 3, I showed that they also turn their profits into free cash flow on a regular basis.

Putting these two things together, a great business will also have consistently high free cash flow returns on capital invested, or CROCI for short. What CROCI is showing us is the free cash flow to the firm as a percentage of capital employed.

CROCI is defined as:

CROCI = adjusted free cash flow to the firm(FCFF)/average capital employed

A CROCI that is consistently over 10% is a sign of a decent business. You may like to use this 10% level as a minimum requirement when you are looking at potential investment candidates. As with ROCE, CROCI is best looked at on a lease-adjusted basis, to get a truer view of a company's financial performance.

I've suggested 10% as a minimum requirement for CROCI, as opposed to the 15% minimum for ROCE earlier in the book. The reason for this is that ROCE is calculated before tax and only deducts depreciation as an expense for fixed assets. CROCI is stated after tax has been paid and all spending on assets (capex) is deducted. In most cases, CROCI will be lower than ROCE.

Table 4.2 shows how to calculate Domino's CROCI for 2015 from its financial statements.

Table 4.2: Calculating Domino's CROCI from its financial statements

Domino's (£m)	2015	2014
Net cash flow from operations	69.0	n/a
Less capex	-6.8	n/a
Dividends from joint ventures	0.5	n/a
Free cash flow to the Firm (FCFF)	62.7	n/a
Total equity	97.7	73.4
Short-term borrowing	1.0	16.1
Non-current liabilities	16.4	14.2
Capital employed	115.1	103.7
Rent/operating lease expense	21.3	20.9
Rents x 7x	149.1	146.3
Lease-adjusted capital employed	264.2	250.0
CROCI calculation		
FCFF	62.7	
Add back lease interest @ 7%	10.4	
Adjusted FCFF	73.1	
Average capital employed	257.1	
CROCI	28.4%	

Now let's look at a couple of real company examples of CROCI.

First, Domino's performs well on the lease-adjusted CROCI measure, as shown in Figure 4.7. Over the ten-year period to the end of 2015, its CROCI was regularly over 15%. It was an impressive 28.4% in 2015.

Domino's ten-year average CROCI has been 18.6%, which is also a good sign. As we have seen with other company data, when looking at measures of company performance it often pays to look at the average values over five to ten years, which may be more representative of a company's sustainable performance than just looking at the latest year's value.

Figure 4.7: Domino's lease-adjusted CROCI (2006–2015)

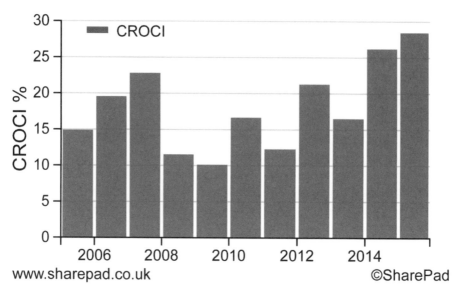

www.sharepad.co.uk   ©SharePad

Looking at another example, the ten-year record of easyJet's lease-adjusted CROCI is shown in Figure 4.8. We saw earlier that easyJet had an impressive lease-adjusted ROCE of 18.6% for 2015. But its CROCI is only 7.9% for 2015. This is lower than my suggested threshold of 10% for CROCI.

That said, we have already identified the potential for easyJet's free cash flow – and therefore also its CROCI – to rise in future years, if its capex is reduced and profits don't fall.

Figure 4.8: easyJet lease-adjusted CROCI (2006–2015)

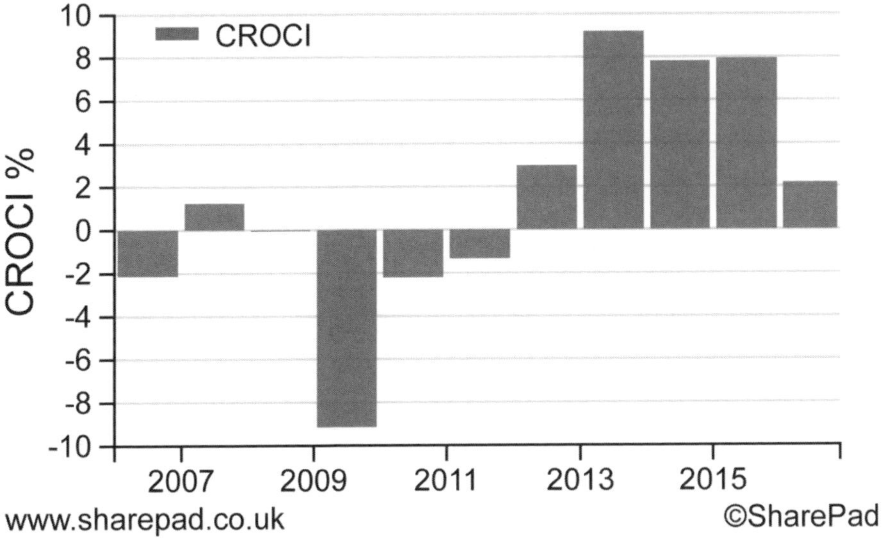

www.sharepad.co.uk   ©SharePad

4. Free cash flow per share

The next way we can use free cash flow is as a tool for checking the quality of a company's profits. Quality companies turn most of their profits into free cash flow on a regular basis.

Over the years the stock market – particularly the smaller companies of the Alternative Investment Market (AIM) – has been littered with companies that seemed to be very profitable but turned out to be anything but. Investors can save themselves a lot of heartache and some painful losses by taking a few minutes to study how effectively a company converts profits into free cash flow.

One of the simplest and best ways to test the quality of a company's profits and whether you think they are believable or not is to compare a company's underlying or normalised earnings per share (EPS) – its profits per share – with its *free cash flow per share (FCFps)*. The free cash flow per share will show you how much surplus cash the company has left over to pay shareholders. It can often be very different from EPS, even though it is supposed to tell you the same thing. For most years, you want to see that free cash flow per share has been close to EPS.

To calculate free cash flow per share for a particular year, you take the free cash flow for shareholders and divide it by the weighted average number of shares in issue. The formula for free cash flow per share is therefore as follows:

free cash flow per share =
free cash flow for shareholders (FCF)/weighted average no of shares in issue

You will find the information for the number of shares in issue in the EPS note to a company's income statement.

Table 4.3 shows the calculation of Domino's free cash flow per share for 2015.

Table 4.3: Calculating Domino's free cash flow per share

Domino's Free cash flow per share calculation	2015 (£m)
Net cash flow from operations	69.0
Capex	-6.8
Dividends from joint ventures	0.5
Free cash flow to the Firm (FCFF)	62.7
Minority or preference dividends paid	0.0
Interest paid	-0.3
Interest received	0.0
Free cash flow for shareholders (FCF)	62.4
Weighted average number of shares in issue	504.6m
Free cash flow per share	12.37p
Underlying EPS	11.9p

Referring to Figure 4.9, we can see that Domino's has performed reasonably well on this test, especially in recent years, which is encouraging.

Figure 4.9: Domino's normalised earnings per share (EPS) and free cash flow per share (FCFps)

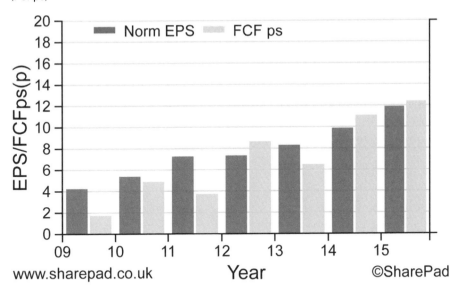

Why earnings per share and free cash flow per share differ

It is important to understand that EPS and free cash flow per share will rarely, if ever, be the same number. Profits are based on smoothing revenues and costs, whereas cash flows tend to be more lumpy. As stated above, what you are looking for in a quality company is for the two numbers to be consistently similar over a period of years. If free cash flow is consistently a lot lower than EPS, this is a warning sign.

The two main reasons for free cash flow being lower than a company's EPS are:

1. *Poor operating cash conversion*: This tends to occur when a company is growing quickly and sells a lot of its goods and services on credit. The profits on these sales get booked in the income statement but there are no cash flows until the customer pays. Companies may also build up stocks or inventories in anticipation of selling more. This is fine as long as the reason is genuine. But building up stocks is also a good way for companies to shift overhead costs such as labour away from the income statement in order to boost profits. This can happen when companies include the overhead costs of producing stock in the balance sheet value. If the stock is unsold at the year-end that overhead cost has not been expensed through the income statement and can therefore boost profits. Selling products on credit can be a sign of overtrading, or even fictitious sales. This sort of thing never turns out well for shareholders, so you need to watch out for this.

2. *High levels of investment in new assets*: This is when capex is much higher than depreciation. Depreciation reduces profits, but money spent on capex reduces free cash flow. In this case, free cash flow per share will be a lot less than EPS. As I mentioned earlier, it is not necessarily a problem for a company to spend heavily on capex, as long as the capex is earning a decent ROCE. However, capex that is consistently much higher than depreciation with no improvement in ROCE is rarely the hallmark of a great company. It can be a sign of dodgy accounting as companies can and do shift expenses into capex to boost profits. easyJet in 2015 is a good example of free cash flow per share being less than earnings per share due to capex being significantly more than depreciation. (Albeit, as we highlighted earlier, this is not a cause for worrying too much about easyJet as the company's ROCE had been increasing at the same time.)

When free cash flow per share is a lot less than EPS it may also be a sign that a company is manipulating its profits to make them look bigger than they really are. In these cases, capex is often much higher than depreciation but the company might be spending this cash just to maintain its existing assets, rather than using the expenditure to enhance its income-producing assets.

In a nutshell, the cash spent should be expensed against revenues and so it should reduce profits. Unless it does this, the depreciation charge reported by the company is probably too low and profits too high. If you are interested to read more about the theory behind this, I discuss this in the section 'How depreciation of assets can distort profit figures' below.

If you are just concerned with the essentials and not worried about the theory then the good news is that for your purposes as a private investor, you don't need to really concern yourself too much with the reasoning behind all of this. The free cash flow per share figure is all-revealing: you want to see quality companies with a consistently similar EPS and FCFps, not companies where these numbers are markedly different.

I find it useful to stick to four simple rules when comparing FCFps with EPS when looking for possible investment candidates:

1. FCFps is 80% or more of EPS = definite candidate

2. FCFps less than 80% of EPS and ROCE is increasing = possible candidate

3. FCFps less than 80% of EPS but ROCE is falling = avoid

4. FCFps is consistently negative = avoid

How depreciation of assets can distort profit figures

Depreciation is an expense that matches the cost of a fixed asset against the revenues it helps to produce. The cost of an asset is spread over its useful life. The most common method of depreciating an asset is known as straight-line depreciation, where an equal amount is charged against revenue over the asset's useful life and is calculated as follows:

straight line depreciation = (cost – residual value)/estimated useful life

So if an asset costs £10 million and will last for 10 years and be worth nothing after that time, the depreciation expensed against revenues for the next ten years will be:

(£10m-£0)/10 years = £1 million per year

Table 4.4 shows how the asset value and depreciation will be reflected in a company's income statement and balance sheet.

Table 4.4: Examples of showing asset value and depreciation over ten years in income statement

Year	Cost	Depreciation expense (income statement)	Accumulated depreciation	Net book value (balance sheet)
1	10	1	1	9
2	10	1	2	8
3	10	1	3	7
4	10	1	4	6
5	10	1	5	5
6	10	1	6	4
7	10	1	7	3
8	10	1	8	2
9	10	1	9	1
10	10	1	10	0

In order to maintain the value of assets at £10 million, the company will have to spend £1 million on new assets each year (the amount it has depreciated by). This is why depreciation is often seen as a proxy for maintenance or stay in business capex. However, the problem with depreciation is that the management of a company can make it whatever value they want. The easiest way to do this is to say that assets will last longer than they will in reality.

What if our £10 million asset only really lasts five years? Depreciation should be £2 million per year instead of £1 million and profits should be £1 million lower. If a company depreciates an asset by £1 million a year but actually spends £2 million to keep the asset up to date, then capex will be twice as much as depreciation but profits will be overstated by £1 million. This will be picked up in the FCFps number but not EPS.

Looking at an example here will help to illustrate the situation.

Sainsbury's, and supermarket companies in general, have consistently spent more on capex than depreciation and produced very low free cash flow per share compared with EPS for many years.

Figure 4.10 shows that Sainsbury's has regularly spent more on capex than its depreciation expense for the period 2006 to 2015. At the same time, it has reported no meaningful growth in profits as measured by EPS.

Figure 4.10: Sainsbury's normalised earnings per share (EPS) and free cash flow per share (FCFps) and capex to depreciation ratio (2006–2015)

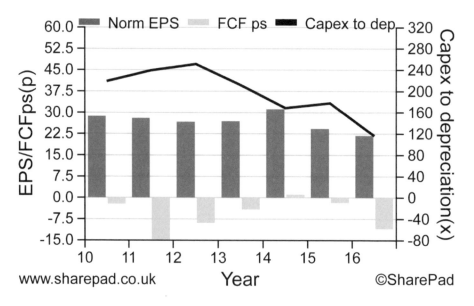

Despite all this investment, EPS has not grown and free cash flow per share has been negative for every one of the ten years in the chart. This begs the question as to how much of the money spent on capex was to grow the business and how much was needed to maintain its existing assets and sales.

If most of this expenditure was actually needed for maintenance, then Sainsbury's depreciation expense may have been too low and its profits too high. Regardless of what the reason is for the high capex, these kind of companies are usually bad investments as they rarely produce enough free cash flow.

The situation shown in Figure 4.10 probably explains why Sainsbury's share price went nowhere over a ten-year period from 2005 and 2015, and why Sainsbury's had to cut its dividend payment to shareholders.

5. Checking the safety of dividend payments

Dividends are an important part of your total return from owning a share. Dividends are a cash payment to you and therefore the company needs to have enough cash flow to make these payments.

You can tell whether a company has sufficient cash to pay dividends by comparing its free cash flow per share with its dividend per share. You can get the dividend per share information from the company's annual report. When you compare these two numbers, you want to see free cash flow per share being the bigger number more often than not.

Occasional years when dividend per share is the larger number are fine, as this may occur when a company is putting cash to good use, such as by investing heavily, but prolonged periods of insufficient free cash flow will often lead to dividends being cut or scrapped eventually.

A quick way to check whether cash flow is sufficient to pay dividends is by using the free cash flow dividend cover ratio. This is calculated as follows:

free cash flow dividend cover = free cash flow per share/dividend per share

If free cash flow is sufficient to pay dividends then the ratio will be more than 1.

When analysing a company, it is a good idea to compare free cash flow per share with dividends per share over a period of ten years. I have done this for Domino's in Figure 4.11.

Domino's free cash flow did not cover its dividend during its period of heavy investment from 2007 to 2010, but since 2012 free cash flow has been more than sufficient to cover dividends. For example, Domino's free cash flow per share in 2015 was 12.4p, whereas its dividend per share was 6.9p; this is a comfortable buffer.

Figure 4.11: Domino's free cash flow per share (FCFps) and dividends per share (DPS)

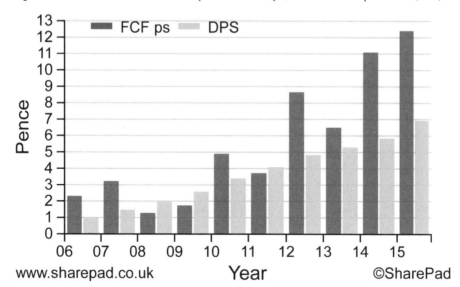

www.sharepad.co.uk   ©SharePad

When free cash flow per share exceeds the dividend per share by a big margin, as it does here, it can be a sign that the company may be capable of paying a much bigger dividend in the future.

6. When free cash flow may not be what it seems

It would be great if we could just follow a simple rule of buying companies that have lots of free cash flow and avoiding the ones that don't. Unfortunately, as with most things in investing, it is not as simple as this. Free cash flow comes with a few caveats that you need to be aware of.

This means that as well as calculating a company's free cash flow, you need to study its cash flow statement closely to really find out what's going on.

Let's look at two examples using real companies so you can better understand what I mean.

British Land – no free cash flow but paying dividends

Using a standard calculation of free cash flow you might be forgiven for thinking that British Land is a basket case. It has produced little or no free cash flow for the ten years from 2006 to 2015, but it has still been paying a dividend. This is shown in Figure 4.12.

How on earth has it been able to do that?

Figure 4.12: British Land free cash flow per share (FCFps) and dividends per share (DPS)

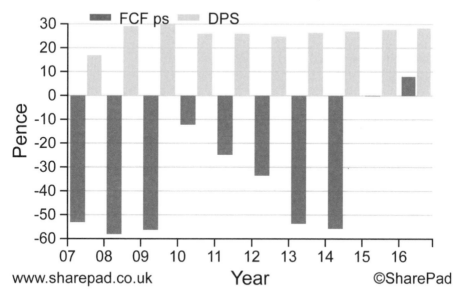

www.sharepad.co.uk ©SharePad

In normal circumstances this situation would be a serious warning sign to avoid the company's shares. But in British Land's case, it might not be. Let's take a closer look at its cash flow statement, in Table 4.5.

Table 4.5: British Land's cash flow statement (2011–2016)

£m unless stated	2011	2012	2013	2014	2015	2016
Cash flows						
Operating profit	830	558	379	1,248	1,941	1,406
Other (operating)	[648]	[283]	[182]	[1,005]	[1,623]	[1,065]
Operating cash flow	182	275	197	243	318	341
Tax paid	-	3	1	-	-	8
Net cash from operations	182	278	198	243	318	349
Capital expenditure	[441]	[488]	[672]	[744]	[329]	[499]
Sale of fixed assets	68	59	699	352	415	564
Acquisitions	[123]	[110]	[318]	[420]	[268]	[241]

£m unless stated	2011	2012	2013	2014	2015	2016
Sale of businesses	22	-	-	197	-	-
Interest received	19	-	31	29	18	11
Other investments received	105	-	74	63	73	58
Dividends from joint ventures	117	-	72	28	134	366
Other (investing)	117	9	[57]	[136]	[231]	[18]
Net cash from investing	[116]	[530]	[171]	[631]	[186]	241
New share issues	-	-	493	11	12	5
New borrowing	171	1,040	393	669	713	717
Repayment of borrowing	[14]	[410]	[889]	[57]	[581]	[919]
Equity dividends paid	[139]	[212]	[203]	[159]	[247]	[235]
Dividends paid to minorities	-	-	-	-	-	[16]
Interest paid	[96]	[89]	[113]	[116]	[124]	[124]
Other (financing)	-	-	290	47	61	[12]
Net cash from financing	[78]	329	[29]	395	[166]	[584]
Net change in cash	**[12]**	**77**	**[2]**	**7**	**[34]**	**6**

British Land owns and builds commercial properties such as offices and shopping centres. As you can see from its cash flow statement, it has been spending a reasonable amount of money on new assets each year, as shown in the capital expenditure line – generally more than the amount of cash that has been coming into the business (its operating cash flow). This is why its free cash flow has been negative.

The standard calculation of free cash flow tends to ignore cash flows that are generated by selling assets and, generally speaking, I agree with excluding these cash flows. This is because selling assets isn't usually a regular and dependable source of cash, compared with trading or operating cash flows.

However, if you are a property company like British Land then making money from selling properties (assets) is a normal part of your day-to-day activities. In this case, it makes sense to consider these sales of assets as part of the free cash flow.

When the asset sales are added back to free cash flow, as in Table 4.6, British Land's performance does not look as bad. If you look at the cumulative figures for the period from 2008–2016, you can see that British Land has sold £4.7bn of assets compared with a cumulative free cash outflow of nearly £2.3bn. When these sales are taken into account, British Land has generated enough cash (£2.4bn) to pay its dividends over the last eight years (£1.7bn). This situation is confirmed by the free cash flow dividend cover ratio, which is 1.42 on average for the eight-year period.

Table 4.6: British Land, free cash flow adjusted for asset sales

British Land (£m)	2008	2009	2010	2011	2012	2013	2014	2015	2016	Cumulative
Free cash flow	−361	−356	−105	−219	−299	−484	−560	17	86	−2281
Add back asset sales	1460	904	279	68	59	699	352	315	564	4700
Adjusted FCF	1099	548	174	−151	−240	215	−208	332	650	2419
Cash dividend cost	161	188	154	139	212	203	159	247	235	1698
FCF dividend cover	6.83	2.91	1.13	−1.09	−1.13	1.06	−1.31	1.34	2.77	1.42

RPS – free cash flow but regularly buying companies

Sometimes you can come across companies that seem to be producing lots of free cash flow when in reality they are not. If you study the investing section of the cash flow statement more closely, large cash outflows might not be found in the capex section but can be found somewhere else, such as acquisitions.

RPS – a consultancy company – appears to generate lots of free cash flow. As it is mainly a people business it has very low capex requirements. However, it does seem to buy other companies every year. If you refer to Table 4.7, you can see this in the 'Acquisitions' row of RPS' financial statement.

Table 4.7: RPS cash flow statement (2010–2015)

£m unless stated	2010	2011	2012	2013	2014	2015
Cash flows						
Operating profit	46.3	42.7	42.1	45.9	50.4	14.9
Depreciation & amortisation	13.1	18.9	19.6	21.6	26.1	28.6
Profit on disposals	[1.6]	0.03	0.02	[0.2]	[0.2]	0.2
Change in stock	-	-	-	-	-	-
Change in debtors	[8]	[3.9]	12.5	8.8	3	29.3
Change in creditors	6.8	12.3	[8.6]	[12]	[11.5]	[2.5]
Change in provisions	-	[10.6]	[0.3]	-	-	20
Change in working capital	[1.2]	[2.2]	3.6	[3.2]	[8.5]	46.8
Other (operating)	1.3	7.9	0.7	0.2	[0.5]	2.1
Operating cash flow	57.9	67.3	66.1	64.3	67.1	92.6

£m unless stated	2010	2011	2012	2013	2014	2015
Tax paid	[14.4]	[12.8]	[18.2]	[19.8]	[19.5]	[11.7]
Net cash from operations	43.5	54.5	47.9	44.5	47.6	80.9
Capital expenditure	[6.9]	[9]	[9.9]	[8]	[7.7]	[8.0]
Sale of fixed assets	3.2	0.4	0.7	0.5	0.5	0.5
Acquisitions	[18]	[17.1]	[9.8]	[31.2]	[37]	[35.4]
Sale of businesses	-	-	0.3	-	-	-
Interest received	0.2	0.3	0.2	0.2	[0.1]	0.2
Dividends from joint ventures	0.1	0.3	-	-	-	-
Other (investing)	0	[5.1]	[4.1]	[3.5]	[19.7]	[16.6]
Net cash from investing	[21.4]	[30.3]	[22.6]	[42]	[63.8]	[59.2]
New share issues	0.2	0.2	0.2	0.6	0.001	-
Share buyback	-	[0.4]	[0.4]	-	-	-
New borrowing	[1.5]	0.8	[1.4]	18	35.8	4.8
Repayment of borrowing	[5]	-	[17.4]	-	-	-
Equity dividends paid	[9.7]	[11.2]	[13]	[15]	[17.4]	[20]
Interest paid	[4.5]	[2.4]	[2.2]	[2]	[3.8]	[6]
Other (financing)	[0.7]	[0.4]	[0.4]	[0.2]	0	[0.2]
Net cash from financing	[21.2]	[13.4]	[34.5]	1.3	14.6	[21.4]
Net change in cash	0.9	10.9	[9.3]	3.8	[1.6]	0.3

In this case, the cash spent on acquisitions should probably be used to calculate free cash flow, in order to give a fair picture.

When this is done for RPS, as in Figure 4.13, its free cash flow is significantly reduced. It looks as if this company is too reliant on buying other companies to produce the cash flow needed to pay its dividend. I would certainly want to investigate this further if I was looking at this company as a potential investment.

Figure 4.13: RPS, free cash flow and free cash flow less acquisitions

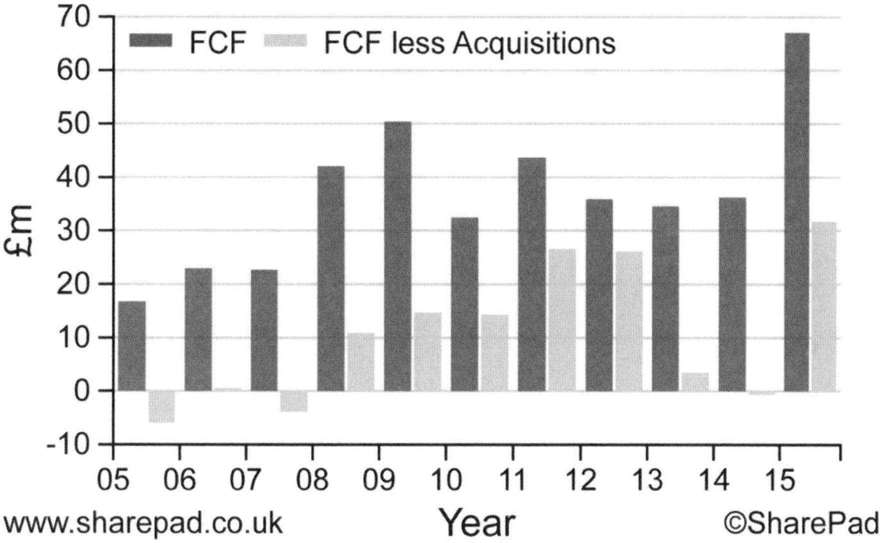

www.sharepad.co.uk   Year   ©SharePad

7. Manipulation of free cash flow

Free cash flow is a popular way to assess a share because investors have become suspicious of company profits. They think – rightly – that profits are too easy to manipulate. Yet, free cash flow can be manipulated as well and you need to know how to spot this.

Companies can boost their free cash flow in many ways. Here are a few ways they can do this:

- *Delay paying their bills until after the end of the financial year*. This increases their trade creditors and boosts operating cash flow and free cash flow for the year.

- *Sell debtors to a credit company*. This is known as debt factoring and allows a company which sells products on credit to turn those sales into cash faster than might have been the case.

- *Cut back on investment*. Slashing investment in new assets can boost free cash flow, but might harm the long-term prospects of the business.

- *Buy businesses rather than invest in new assets*: A standard calculation of free cash flow might ignore this.

This is why you should review a company's free cash flow over a number of years (I suggest at least five) and look at the trend. You need to look at what is causing free cash flow to change, as not all free cash flow should be valued the same.

Ideally, a company should be generating more free cash flow because its profits are growing. This is the highest quality of free cash flow. Companies that are boosting cash flows through changes in working capital (paying their bills later, collecting their debtors faster and holding less stocks of finished goods) or cutting capex might be doing the right thing, but these kind of improvements are not achievable year after year.

PART 1 SUMMARY

HOW TO FIND QUALITY COMPANIES

Now that I have introduced the ways to find quality companies by analysing financial statements, let's summarise what we have learned, to provide a useful checklist you can use when you are searching for quality companies.

1. Look at the company's sales record. You want to see high and growing sales, year after year. A ten-year period of increasing sales and profits is a good sign.

2. Look at the company's profits. You want to see high and growing profits, as measured by normalised EBIT, year after year. A ten-year period of increasing sales and profits is a good sign.

3. Check that reported EBIT and normalised EBIT are roughly the same in most of the last ten years.

4. Look for the company to have a profit margin – in the form of EBIT margin – of at least 10% almost every year for the last ten years.

5. Look for the company to have a ROCE that is consistently above 15% over the last ten years.

6. Carry out a DuPont analysis to find out what is driving a company's ROCE.

7. Read a company's annual report to provide context for the numbers.

8. Look for a growing free cash flow to the firm (FCFF) and free cash flow for shareholders (FCF), over a period of ten years. FCFF and FCF should also be roughly the same in most years.

9. Look for companies that turn all of their operating profit into operating cash flow, as represented by an operating cash conversion ratio of 100% or higher.

10. Look for a capex ratio less than 30% almost every year over the last ten years.

11. If the company is spending more on capex than its depreciation and amortisation expenses, it is a sign that it is spending enough, but you need to be sure it isn't spending too much.

12. Check for free cash flow return on capital invested (CROCI) that is higher than 10% almost every year over the last ten years.

13. Look for free cash flow per share to be close to earnings per share in most of the last ten years.

14. Free cash flow per share should be a larger number than dividend per share in most years (the free cash flow dividend cover should be greater than 1). Occasional years when this is not the case are fine.

15. Prefer more consistent growth in turnover and profit to more volatile growth.

Don't worry if you cannot find a company that meets all of the criteria above. There are some exceptional companies that do, but typically you will not find hundreds of them. However, companies can improve and ones that might not have been good ten years ago can be good companies now. If you can find companies that have a high and improving ROCE and have been good at converting profits into free cash flow over the last five years, you should consider them as well.

In Appendix 2 at the end of the book I have included a table showing the results of FTSE 100 companies for several of these quality measures. This serves to show you how many quality companies there are and also the kinds of results that companies are delivering on these measures.

PART 2

HOW TO AVOID DANGEROUS COMPANIES

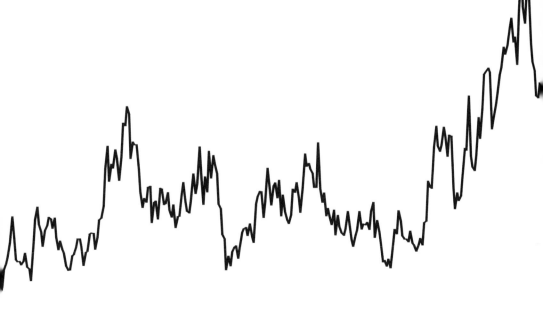

PART 2 – HOW TO AVOID DANGEROUS COMPANIES

Picking winning shares is something that every investor naturally wants to do.

However, success in investing is just as much about avoiding bad investments and minimising the risks that you take with your money.

In my experience, investors spend far too much time thinking about how much money they can potentially make from owning a share and not enough time thinking about how much money they could lose if things go wrong.

The reason why avoiding bad investments is so important is because they are hard to recover from. If you lose 50% of your money invested, you need to find an investment that will double in value just to get the value of your portfolio back to where it started. Therefore, the more bad investments you can avoid, the better your long-term investment performance is likely to be.

So how do you stay away from bad investments?

The first thing you can do is focus your investments on quality companies with the following characteristics:

- A consistent track record of increasing sales and profits.

- High returns on capital employed (ROCE).

- An ability to turn a high proportion of profits into free cash flow.

We have covered this already in Part 1. In Part 2, we look at arguably the biggest danger that shareholders face when investing in a business – debt. We look at three different types of debt:

1. Borrowed money from banks and investors. This is known as total borrowings.

2. Hidden debts that come from companies renting rather than owning assets.

3. Pension fund deficits. These can be very significant debt-like liabilities that can do a lot of damage to the value of a company's shares.

In Part 2 you will learn how to analyse a company's debts so that you can distinguish between safe and dangerous companies. This will help you to stay away from risky investments that have the potential to damage your wealth.

5

THE DANGERS OF DEBT

WHEN A COMPANY borrows money from lenders to finance its business, it is in debt to them until the money is repaid. The words borrowing and debt are interchangeable with each other when it comes to a company's finances.

Investors should not automatically worry if a company has debt, because often debt can be a good thing. You will find most companies have some form of debt. Borrowing money from banks or investors to finance part of a company's business is perfectly normal. In fact, it has advantages over money that has been invested by shareholders. Because debt is often secured against the value of a company's assets – like a mortgage on a property – and lenders get paid interest before shareholders get paid dividends, debt is a cheaper form of finance than shareholder or equity finance. Interest payments also lower a company's tax bill. It's when a company has too much debt that it becomes a problem.

In this chapter, I explain why too much debt increases the risk that shareholders will lose money. I cover concepts such as financial gearing as well as how to scrutinise a company's debts. I also look at how to recognise when debt could be a problem and when it is nothing to worry about.

As I show, ideally you should look to invest in companies with no debt, or very little debt relative to their capital employed and profits.

The risk of debt: shareholders get paid last

A company has three main choices when it comes to financing its business. It can get money from shareholders (equity), use the profits and free cash flows produced by the company, or it can borrow from lenders.

It is worth understanding that debt can be good for a company's shareholders. If a company uses the money it has borrowed and invests it wisely in profitable projects, it can earn enough money to pay the interest on the debt, repay the loan over time and leave a growing pile of money for its shareholders.

The problems with debt tend to occur when a company borrows too much to invest in poor projects and ends up with too much debt and too much interest to pay relative to its profits and cash flows. This matters for shareholders because lenders have to be paid before them.

Unlike dividends, interest payments on debt are not optional. Failure to make these payments will mean the company risks being declared bankrupt. Therefore, the larger a company's debt, the larger the interest bill, which means more risk for shareholders of not being paid. This is because the more interest a company has to pay, the bigger slice of trading profits it will eat up and the less cash will be left over to pay shareholders. If trading profits fall then there might not be any money left over for dividends.

This risk is explained by something known as *financial gearing*.

Understanding financial gearing

The best way to understand the risk of debt to shareholders is to show how it can have a big impact on the profits made for them. The interest on debt *magnifies* the changes in shareholder profits that result from a change in sales. This is known as financial gearing.

Just as a higher gear on a bike means that you can travel further with each turn of the pedals, more debt and more interest has a bigger impact on profits for each percentage change in sales. This is great when things are going well and sales are growing, but it is not so good when times are tough and sales are falling.

Let's have a look at an example.

Let's compare two identical companies with identical amounts of money invested of £1bn, both earning £200m in trading profits a year (meaning a ROCE of 20%).

Company A has no debt. Company B has lots of debt: it has chosen to finance its £1bn of assets with £800m of debt with an interest rate of 10% and £200m of shareholders' equity. Company B therefore has a £80m interest bill to pay every year.

Looking at Company A first.

Company A

£m	Normal	Good	Bad
Sales	1000	1200	800
Sales % change		20%	−20%
EBIT	200	240	160
Sales % change		20%	−20%
Interest	0	0	0
Profit before tax	200	240	160
Taxation @ 20%	−40	−48	−32
Profit for shareholders	160	192	128
Profit for shareholders % change		20%	−20%

Company A turns £1bn of sales into £200m of EBIT and £160m of profit for shareholders after taxation at a rate of 20% has been paid. To keep things very simple, I've assumed that the percentage change in sales will feed through to the same percentage change in EBIT just to illustrate financial gearing.

This won't be the same in the real world as companies have operating costs which are fixed and don't change when sales change. This gives rise to *operational gearing*, which we looked at in an earlier chapter. To recap, it means that for a given percentage change in sales there will be a bigger percentage change in trading profits.

The easiest way to spot a company with high operational gearing is to look at the track record of its turnover and trading profits. If you see that profits move up and down a lot over a long period of time that is usually a telling sign. As I mentioned earlier, buying companies with stable profits and profit margins reduces your risk as an investor.

NOTE: Don't get caught out by the similar terms – *operational gearing* and *financial gearing* are different concepts. Operational gearing is the change in profits caused by fixed operating costs and financial gearing is the change in profits caused by fixed interest costs.

As you can see with the case of Company A, with no financial gearing, the change in profits for shareholders mirrors the percentage change in sales. A 20% change in sales leads to a 20% change in profits. Even when sales fall by 20% in the bad scenario, there is still £128m of profit for shareholders.

Company B

For Company B, the existence of debt and interest payments gears the change in profits for shareholders coming from a change in sales, because the £80m of interest has to be paid come what may.

£m	Normal	Good	Bad
Sales	1000	1200	800
Sales % change		20%	−20%
EBIT	200	240	160
EBIT % change		20%	−20%
Interest @ 10%	−80	−80	−80
Profit before tax	120	160	80
Taxation @ 20%	−24	−32	−16
Profit for shareholders	96	128	64
Profit for shareholders % change		33%	−33%

Here, a 20% increase in sales in the good scenario leads to a 33% change in profits. That's fine when times are good. However, during bad times shareholders take a big hit. Company B's shareholders end up with half as much money as Company A's when sales are reduced by 20% (£128m compared to £64m).

This is why debt can be very dangerous for shareholders, particularly in the case of cyclical companies whose sales have a tendency to move up and down a lot in line with the general economy or commodity prices. If sales and profits are fluctuating, returns for shareholders are not stable and predictable.

This serves as a reminder that investing in quality companies which are not subject to big falls in sales and trading profits is the cornerstone of successful long-term investing.

Measuring a company's debt

It is relatively easy to measure the amount of debt a company has by calculating some simple ratios. There are lots of ratios which can be used to explain a company's debt position, but for most investors the following four will tell you what you need to know:

1. Debt to free cash flow.

2. Debt to net operating cash flow.

3. Debt to assets.

4. Interest cover.

These ratios only deal with debt shown on a company's balance sheet. I will deal with hidden, or off-balance sheet, debts in the next chapter.

Let's look at each of these ratios in turn.

1. Debt to free cash flow

Debt to free cash flow tells you how many years it would take to repay all a company's debt with the current rate of free cash flow it is producing. The lower the number, the better, as a lower number means that a company can repay its debt quickly. I would rarely look at a company with a ratio that has been consistently more than 10. Debt to free cash flow is calculated as follows:

debt to free cash flow = total borrowings/free cash flow

This ratio can give a high number for two reasons: high debt or low free cash flow. It will give a negative number if a company has negative free cash flow.

Like all ratios, it is best looked at over a number of years to see if it is normal for a company to have a high value or if it is a recent trend.

Table 5.1 shows companies with high levels of debt to free cash flow based on their 2015 or 2016 annual accounts. Property, pubs and utility companies normally have high levels of debt as they are deemed to have sufficiently stable cash flows to support it.

The data in the table shows that Rolls-Royce would take over 200 years to repay its debts based on its current free cash flows. As Figure 5.1 shows, this is not normal given its recent history and would suggest that you need to investigate what is going on. For example, has debt surged or has free cash flow plummeted? Does the management have a plan to reduced debt and increase free cash flow?

Table 5.1: Companies with very high debt to free cash flow ratios

Name	Debt to FCF
Rolls-Royce Group	229.7
BP	141.7
NCC Group	131.1
Intu Properties	67.9
Greene King	47.9
G4S	45.6
British Land Co	43.2
UNITE Group	39.6
Mitchells & Butlers	39.5
Severn Trent	39.1
Thomas Cook Group	38.4
SSE	32.8
Greencore Group	30.0
Big Yellow Group	29.5
National Grid	28.3

Figure 5.1: Rolls-Royce debt to free cash flow (2007–2015)

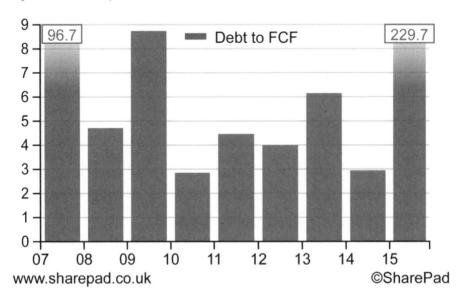

By contrast, the companies in Table 5.2 have enough free cash flow to pay off all their borrowings in a matter of months.

Table 5.2: Companies with low debt to free cash flow ratios

Name	Debt to FCF
Bovis Homes Group	0.03
CMC Markets	0.03
Aveva Group	0.04
JD Sports Fashion	0.04
Computacenter	0.08
Elementis	0.09
Bodycote	0.09
Cranswick	0.10
Diploma	0.18
Burberry Group	0.19
Domino's Pizza UK & IRL	0.20
Bellway	0.20
Taylor Wimpey	0.25
Barratt Developments	0.26
Wizz Air Holding	0.29

2. Debt to net operating cash flow

Net operating cash flow is the amount of cash a company has from trading after it has paid its taxes. By comparing this number with the total amount of debt, you can see how long it would take the company to pay back the debt if it stopped investing in its assets. Again, the lower the number, the better. It is calculated as follows:

debt to net operating cash flow = total borrowings/net operating cash flow

This is a worst-case scenario test. You should remember that this ratio assumes the company spends nothing at all on maintaining its assets for a period of time. This can only happen for a couple of years for most companies before their assets become worn out and lose their ability to make money.

Therefore, with most companies I'd argue that you wouldn't really want to see a debt to net operating cash flow ratio of more than 3. Property, pubs and utility companies – as we have seen above – would tend to have higher values. Table 5.3 shows a selection of companies with high ratios in 2016.

Table 5.3: Companies with high debt to free cash flow ratios

Name	Debt/net opcf
Marston's	8.0
AA	7.8
SIG	7.2
Crest Nicholson Holdings	6.7
GlaxoSmithKline	6.5
Greene King	6.5
Severn Trent	6.4
Antofagasta	6.4
Ultra Electronics Holdings	6.3
Cobham	6.3
Mitchells & Butlers	6.3
Carillion	6.0
Vedanta Resources	5.6
Rolls-Royce Group	5.4
Ascential	5.4
RPC Group	5.4
Daejan Holdings	5.3
Tesco	5.3
National Grid	5.3
BAE Systems	5.2

Once you are starting to get a value for this ratio of over 5, you are looking at companies with significant amounts of debt relative to their cash flows. Marston's and AA for example, look to be extremely risky. Mining companies such as Antofagasta and Tesco are on this list in 2016 as their profits and cash flows have been weak, which has increased their financial risk.

3. Debt to assets

Debt to assets is very much like a loan-to-value measure on a house. It tells you what percentage of a company's assets is taken up by debt. The higher the percentage, the more risky a company generally is. It is calculated as follows:

debt to assets = total borrowings/total assets

Generally speaking, I tend to avoid companies where the debt to total assets ratio is more than 50%. This is one of the reasons why shares of banks can be extremely risky, as debt to assets ratios are over 90% in 2016.

Domino's on-balance sheet debt is a very low percentage of its total assets, which is a good sign. At the end of 2015 Domino's had £12.4m of total borrowings and £185.4m of total assets, giving a very low debt to total assets ratio of 6.7%.

4. Interest cover

Interest cover is not a measure of debt, but a measure of how many times a company's annual trading profits can pay the interest on its debt. The higher the number, the safer the company is. Interest cover is calculated as follows:

interest cover = EBIT/interest payable

I look for a figure of at least five times, but prefer to invest in companies where the ratio is 10 or more.

Excluding utility companies and property companies which have high levels of debt – and therefore low interest cover – a figure of five means that profits can fall by at least 40% before the ratio starts getting into the danger zone, which I define as interest cover of three or less.

Using debt ratios to analyse companies

When I am analysing a company's debt, I make the necessary calculations for all four of the debt ratios and view them alongside each other. I have done this for a sample of five companies in Table 5.4.

How do you analyse the results in this table?

It is clear that Domino's has very low levels of debt on its balance sheet. It could repay all its borrowings in less than three months based on its current free cash flow and it has no problems paying the interest on it. On this basis, this is a kind of company I might want to own shares in.

Table 5.4: The debt measure ratios for five companies

Name	Debt to OPCF	Debt / FCF	Interest cover	Debt/total assets
AA	7.8	22.9	1.8	162.0%
Domino's Pizza UK & IRL	0.2	0.2	213.9	6.7%
Greene King	6.5	47.9	3.1	43.3%
InterContinental Hotels	2.5	4.1	6.8	44.3%
Severn Trent	6.4	39.1	2.5	58.1%

Other companies in the table have much higher levels of debt. The AA's debt would take nearly 23 years to pay back. Its profits cover its interest payments less than twice. This kind of situation represents a risk of going bankrupt if profits were to deteriorate. This would be enough to put me off buying its shares.

Pub companies such as Greene King are frequently financed with high levels of debt. These companies can also tend to be quite poor at producing lots of free cash flow, as they have to keep spending money to keep their pubs in good condition. This makes them quite risky investments for shareholders when times get tough and profits fall. These companies are often forced to sell their assets – pubs – to repay debts.

Water companies such as Severn Trent are financed with lots of debt. This is not usually a problem given that they have very stable and predictable profits and cash flows. Water is not the kind of product that tends to see demand change if the economy changes. However, if you are building a portfolio of quality companies with high free cash flows and ROCE then it is unlikely that you will own shares of water companies. This is because the returns they can earn are capped by industry regulators, which means they have very low ROCE.

InterContinental Hotels looks to be conservatively financed and meets my target debt criteria.

Different types of debt

As well as understanding the risk of too much debt, you need to appreciate that companies can have different types of debt with different implications for shareholders. In this section we consider the following types of debt:

1. Fixed rate debt.

2. Floating rate debt.

The best way to understand this is to look at some examples of company borrowings, which you will find in their annual reports. You can find the information on a company's borrowings in the notes to its accounts. As an example, Table 5.5 shows a breakdown of the borrowings of Imperial Brands (formerly Imperial Tobacco).

Table 5.5: Imperial Brands' borrowings

£m	2015	2014
Current borrowings		
Bank loans and overdrafts	53	108
Capital market issuance:		
European commercial paper (ECP)	359	321
€500m 4.0% notes due December 2015	380	-
€1,500m 8.375% notes due February 2016	1,165	-
Total current borrowings	**1,957**	**429**
Non-current borrowings		
Bank loans	1,479	-
Capital market issuance:		
€500m 4.0% notes due December 2015	-	394
€1,500m 8.375% notes due February 2016	-	1,226
£450m 5.5% notes due November 2016	471	471
$1,250m 2.05% notes due February 2018	825	773
€850m 4.5% notes due July 2018	634	667
$500m 2.05% notes due July 2018	330	-
£200m 6.25% notes due December 2018	210	210
£500m 7.75% notes due June 2019	510	510
€750m 5.0% notes due December 2019	576	606
$1,250m 2.95% notes due July 2020	826	-
€1,000m 2.25% notes due Feburary 2021	745	785
£1,000m 9.0% notes due February 2022	1,054	1,054
$1,250m 3.75% notes due July 2022	827	-
$1,000m 3.5% notes due February 2023	660	618
£600m 8.125% notes due March 2024	626	626
$1,500m 4.25% notes due July 2025	986	-

£m	2015	2014
€650m 3.375% notes due February 2026	488	514
£500m 5.5% notes due September 2026	499	499
£500m 4.875% notes due June 2032	504	509
Total non-current borrowings	12,250	9,462
Total borrowings	14,207	9,891
Analysed as:		
Capital market issuance:	12,675	9,783
Bank loans and overdrafts	1,532	108

Here we can see that Imperial had £14,207m (£14.2bn) of total borrowings outstanding at the end of 2015. Its current borrowings – money which has to be paid back within one year – were £1.96bn, with non-current borrowings of £12.25bn.

The first thing to notice is that the company has a mix of debt. It has borrowed some money from banks but most of its borrowed money has come from investors in its bonds, which it calls 'capital market issuance'.

The company says that the bank loans and overdrafts pay floating rates of interest. This means they are likely to rise and fall with general interest rates (e.g. Bank of England rate or LIBOR). Floating rate debt can be helpful and boost a company's profits and free cash flow when interest rates are falling, but it can cause problems when interest rates are rising because debt becomes more expensive.

This is why many companies choose to borrow at fixed rates of interest. It gives them and their shareholders a high level of certainty regarding how much interest will have to be paid each year and when the loan will have to be paid back. Personally, I like to see companies with lots of borrowing at fixed rates of interest. It means that there is less uncertainty and risk if interest rates rise. From an investor's point of view, it is very similar to a person with a fixed-rate mortgage. They have certainty on how much they will be paying for a set period of time.

For example, right at the bottom of Imperial's borrowing note you can see it has a £500m bond outstanding, paying an annual interest rate of 4.875% (£24.38m each year), and which has to be paid back in 2032.

Keep an eye on the interest rates being paid on individual bonds and when they have to be paid back. As the maturity date of the bond approaches and the money is due to be repaid, ask yourself whether a company will be able to replace that bond with a new one at a higher or lower interest rate.

It is not uncommon for some companies to have bonds that were issued back in the 1990s when interest rates were a lot higher than they are in 2016. If the bond represents a significant part of total borrowings, the lower interest costs from replacing a maturing bond can give a nice boost to profits and free cash flow. This process can work in reverse when bonds with low interest rates are replaced when interest rates are rising. You can easily find free market data on historic interest rates – the Bank of England website is a good place to look – to help you work out the direction in which interest rates have moved since the company issued a bond.

Imperial is borrowing at interest rates between 2.05% and 9%. The bonds issued in pounds have some of the highest interest rates and these might be able to be replaced at a cheaper interest rate in the future.

You will also notice that Imperial has borrowed in different currencies. It has bonds outstanding which are denominated in pounds, euros and US dollars. This makes a lot of sense given that a large chunk of a company's assets are located in those currencies.

However, you should watch out for currency mismatching. This can occur when a company has a much bigger percentage of its borrowings in one currency than its assets or profits in that currency. Sometimes a company can be tempted to borrow money in a foreign currency with low interest rates where it has little or no profits. If the exchange rate changes, and the value of the loan and the interest expense rises when it is translated back into pounds, the company's profits can take a hit.

Let me show how this can play out in practice.

Let's say a UK company borrows $500m at an interest rate of 5%. It will pay $25m a year in interest. If a British pound buys $1.50 then this will be £16.7m when the interest paid is converted into pounds.

If the value of the pound falls to $1.20 then the interest paid in pounds will increase by 25%, as shown in Table 5.6.

Table 5.6: The effect of a changing exchange rate on foreign borrowings

Borrowings (m)	$500	$500
Interest @ 5% (m)	$25	$25
Exchange rate	£1 = $1.50	£1 = $1.20
Interest (m)	£16.67	£20.83

This is not a problem if the company has profits in US dollars as they will have increased in value when converted back into pounds. A problem can occur if a company has a bigger proportion of its total loans in a foreign currency than it does profits. This is not the case with Imperial, but it is something you should look out for in a company.

When does the debt have to be paid back?

During the financial crisis of 2008–09, there was a real fear that companies would not be able to gain access to new loans when existing ones had to be paid back. Situations like this can have big, negative implications for companies with lots of short-term debt.

In the worst-case scenario, companies might not be able to repay the debt that is due with a new loan. They might be forced to sell assets or ask shareholders for money instead. Or they might be granted a new loan, but at a much higher interest rate.

Another potentially risky situation is when interest rates are rising and the company has large chunks of debts that it needs to replace rather than pay off. This increases the possibility that the new loans will have higher interest rates attached to them, which in turn will depress profits and free cash flows for shareholders.

As an investor you can monitor this risk by looking at the company's debt repayment schedule in the notes to its accounts. For example, in Table 5.7 we can see that for Imperial a very small chunk of its borrowings has to be repaid within two years and so the risk of a nasty surprise would appear to be quite low.

Table 5.7: Imperial's debt repayment schedule

	2015			2014 (Restated)		
£m	Borrowings	Net derivative financial liabilities/ (assets)	Total	Borrowings	Net derivative financial liabilities/ (assets)	Total
Amounts maturing:						
Between one and two years	1,457	67	1,524	1,620	[47]	1,573
Between two and five years	4,405	[127]	4,278	2,631	26	2,657
In five years or more	6,388	[106]	6,282	5,211	61	5,272
	12,250	[166]	12,084	9,462	40	9,502

If a company has a large amount of debt maturing in the near term this is a warning sign for an investor. Good companies will manage the repayment schedule of their borrowings – known as maturity risk – so that they do not have to repay and replace large chunks of debt at the same time.

When larger debts are not a problem

In an ideal world, you will be selecting companies to invest in that produce consistently high returns and have low levels of debt. This is the essence of quality and safe investing. But does this mean that all companies with large amounts of debt should be avoided?

Not necessarily.

There are some companies which can cope with higher levels of debt and still potentially make good investments. These are companies with very stable and predictable profits and cash flows. A good example is funeral provider Dignity plc.

Sadly, life does not last forever and all of us will die one day. Whilst death rates do vary from year to year, they are unlikely to collapse. This makes the business of providing funerals one of the most predictable businesses there is. This has given Dignity some very favourable profit and cash flow characteristics, as shown in Table 5.8.

Table 5.8: Dignity's profit, cash flow and debt figures

£m unless stated	2010	2011	2012	2013	2014	2015
Financial performance and debt						
Turnover	199.1	210.1	229.6	256.7	268.9	305.3
EBIT	61.0	64.5	69.4	76.8	85.9	98.7
FCF	12.1	15.2	29.1	36.9	49.8	72.7
EBIT margin	30.6	30.7	30.2	29.9	31.9	32.3
ROCE	16.0	15.9	16.3	13.0	14.8	16.2
CROCI	9.3	10.1	12.7	11.0	13.5	16.1
Debt/FCF	28.7	22.3	11.3	13.1	12.3	8.3
Debt/Net OPCF	5.6	5.4	4.5	5.9	6.4	5.1
Debt/Total Assets	83.9	80.1	71.3	77.4	101.4	89.2
Interest cover	2.8	2.7	2.9	2.8	2.9	3.7

As you can see, Dignity has had a consistently high debt to total assets ratio and quite low levels of interest cover. Yet it has managed to produce many of the hallmarks of a quality company. It has grown its sales ('Turnover' row), profits ('EBIT' row) and free cash flows ('FCF' row) whilst maintaining high profit margins ('EBIT margin' row) and very good levels of ROCE and CROCI.

The general point here is that if a company shows it can continue to increase turnover and EBIT – sales and profit – year after year, whilst holding high levels of debt, then this can still be regarded as a quality company and potentially a good investment.

Having now looked at the dangers of debt, in Chapter 6 we move on to look at how debt can make you think a company is performing better than it really is.

6

HOW DEBT CAN FOOL YOU

D EBT CAN FOOL you into thinking a company is performing better than it really is. In this chapter you will see how that can happen and how you can avoid getting tricked.

Financial engineering

A company can use debt to paint a distorted picture of its finances.

Let's look at an example to see how this works.

Bob's Book Shop is a very steady business that has been built up over decades. It makes a £100m in trading profits (or EBIT) each year. It does not like taking financial risk and therefore has no debt. All the company's assets are financed with shareholders' equity and reinvested profits. The situation is shown in Table 6.1.

Table 6.1: Bob's Book Shop financial situation

Bob's Book Shop (£m)	Before (shareholders' equity, no debt)	After (debt replaces £800m of equity)	Change
Sales	1000	1000	0%
EBIT	100	100	0%
Interest @ 6%	0	−48	
Profit before tax	100	52	−48%
Taxation @ 20%	−20	−10.4	−48%
Profit after tax	80	41.6	−48%

Bob's Book Shop (£m)	Before (shareholders' equity, no debt)	After (debt replaces £800m of equity)	Change
Equity	1000	200	−80%
Debt	0	800	
Total Capital	1000	1000	0%
ROCE	10%	10%	0%
ROE	8%	21%	160%

Selling books is a competitive business and so it does not make particularly high returns. Its return on capital (ROCE) is a modest 10% and return on equity (ROE) is 8%. (ROE is calculated as the profit the business makes as a percentage of shareholder equity, thus £80m of post-tax profit is 8% of £1000m shareholder equity.)

The company is approached by an investment banker. He says the company has too much equity financing and not enough debt. He reckons that by taking on more debt and reducing the equity financing, the company could transform the way it looks to investors. The table above shows how the company's financial statement looks before, with no debt, and after, with £800m of debt at an interest rate of 6%.

By replacing £800m of equity with £800m of debt, the ROE would more than double to 21%. (£41.6m of profit after tax is 21% of £200m shareholder equity.)

What's not to like about this?

Quite a lot actually.

What's being described here is a case of financial engineering. It is important to understand that apart from the way the company is financed, nothing else has changed.

EBIT and ROCE have not changed

The company's trading profits are still £100m and there is still £1000m of total capital invested. This means ROCE is still 10%.

Why debt increases ROE

ROE has gone up because the percentage fall in post-tax profits caused by the interest payments on the debt is smaller than the percentage change in shareholders' equity.

What I mean by this is that pre-tax profits have fallen by the £48m of interest (6% of £800m), but because of this the company pays less tax. It pays £10.4m instead of £20m before. Post-tax profits have fallen by 48%. But the amount of shareholders' equity has fallen by 80%, as £800m of it has been swapped for £800m of debt. This has had the effect of increasing the ROE because profits have fallen by less than the amount of shareholders' equity.

However, it is clear that this is just because of the change in the way the company has been financed. The underlying productivity of the company's assets and total capital are still making a 10% return – this has not changed. You should not be fooled by what is going on here. By focusing on ROCE, not ROE, you will not be fooled by a company taking on more debt.

The risk to shareholders has increased considerably

We know that ROE has gone up but ROCE has not changed at all. We should also note that the risk to shareholders has increased too, because of all the extra debt.

Table 6.2 shows the changes in the company's borrowing levels and interest cover after the debt has been taken on.

Table 6.2: Changes in borrowing levels and interest cover before and after debt

	Before debt	After debt
Interest cover	N/A	2.08
Debt to total assets	0	80%

We can see that the ability of the company to pay its interest bills as measured by its interest cover is quite thin. The interest bill is only covered twice by profits. A fall in profits could make paying the interest bill more difficult and would leave less money to pay shareholders.

Debt now accounts for 80% of the company's assets or total capital. A fall in the value of those assets would also see a big hit to the value of shareholders' equity, as the amount of debt would be a higher proportion of total assets. Remember that the value of equity is essentially the value of assets less debt. If asset values fall and debt levels stay the same, the value of what is left over – the equity – will fall.

Now, having looked at how debt can fool investors, we move on to look at a very important and often overlooked subject – hidden debts.

7

HIDDEN DEBTS

How to analyse companies with hidden debts

THE METHODS I introduce in this chapter can be regarded as quite advanced financial analysis. However, if you are thinking of investing in the shares of airline, rail or retail companies, and many others, then you need to understand one of the biggest risks that you will face as a shareholder – hidden debts.

By understanding what hidden debts are and how to analyse companies that have them, you will make better investment decisions and take on less risk.

So, what are hidden debts?

Hidden debts are debt-like liabilities that are not shown on a company's balance sheet in the same way as a bank loan or underfunded pension fund would be. Diligent investors need to take hidden debts into account when analysing and valuing companies.

The most common example of hidden, off-balance-sheet debt is something known as an operating lease. Examples of operating leases are rents paid by retailers for their stores, airlines for their aeroplanes and by rail companies for their locomotives and carriages. In all these cases, the companies commit to rent these assets for an agreed period of time and then return them to their owners at the end of the contract.

The presence of rents or operating leases in a company's finances can have big implications for investors. If you ignore these kinds of payments, you can mistakenly think that a company is better or safer than it really is.

In this chapter, I describe what you need to know to analyse companies with large hidden debts. I use the example of Domino's to illustrate the practical analysis tools that you might need to use.

Domino's and its hidden debts

When you are analysing a company that has a number of stores or other large assets – such as Domino's, or the airlines or rail companies I have already mentioned – one of the first things you should do is check out whether it rents rather than owns these assets. In the case of Domino's, we are checking to see if it rents or owns its pizza shops.

Why do we do this?

Well, because the commitment to keep on renting these shops in the future can represent a big liability that isn't disclosed on a company's balance sheet. Effectively, it is hidden from view and is only found by digging deeply into a company's accounts.

Let me explain why this matters to an investor.

A company such as Domino's has two choices when looking to pay for a new shop. It can pay for the whole cost itself upfront from its cash reserves or by borrowing money. Alternatively, it can rent it from a property company or landlord. If it buys or builds a shop itself and pays for it with a bank loan, this is how it is shown in the company's accounts:

On the balance sheet, the cost of the building is added to assets. The bank loan to pay for it is added to liabilities. In the income statement, trading profits (or EBIT) will be stated after depreciating the asset over its useful life. Pre-tax profits will then be stated after this extra depreciation and the extra interest costs on the bank loan. The free cash flow of the company in the year(s) the store was built would be reduced by the total cost of building it (capex).

If Domino's rents the shop instead, something different happens. The company will typically enter into an agreement with a landlord to rent a building for an agreed period of time – typically five, ten or even 25 years. Domino's usually won't be able to get out of this agreement before the end of the agreed term without negotiating a payment to the owners, which could be as much as the total of the remaining rent.

Every year it rents the store, Domino's expenses the annual rent against its income. These rents are known as operating leases. No asset or liability is entered on its balance sheet. There is no cash outflow, apart from the rent. So free cash flow looks a lot better in the first year than if the store had been paid for in full. However, this is not a free lunch, because the company has signed up to pay a lot of rent in the future.

Accountants have been arguing about these kinds of rents for years. Many say that because companies like Domino's are committed to paying rents, those commitments are a liability just like a loan. Also, the benefit of using the rented store should be seen as an asset. So both the store asset and the liability for future rents should be shown on the balance sheet.

By not doing this, companies are essentially hiding debt-like liabilities and understating their financial risks. This is why I refer to this situation has *hidden debt*. A company's return on capital employed (ROCE) will also be overstated, because the obligation to pay future rents is not on the balance sheet and therefore not part of capital employed.

You can find a company's future rent obligations (often referred to as non-cancellable operating leases) buried in the notes at the back of their accounts. Table 7.1 shows Domino's operating lease commitments as of December 2015.

Table 7.1: Domino's operating lease commitments (December 2015)

	At 27 December 2015 £000	At 28 December 2014 £000
Not later than one year	20,386	19,696
After one year but not more than five years	71,954	72,060
After five years	128,865	140,770
Total	221,205	232,526

As you can see, Domino's is on the hook for over £221m of future rent payments. This is a big number which is not on its balance sheet. The outstanding operating leases have been growing significantly in recent years, as the number of shops Domino's trades from has increased. This trend is shown in Figure 7.1.

Figure 7.1: Domino's increasing operating lease commitments (2010–2015)

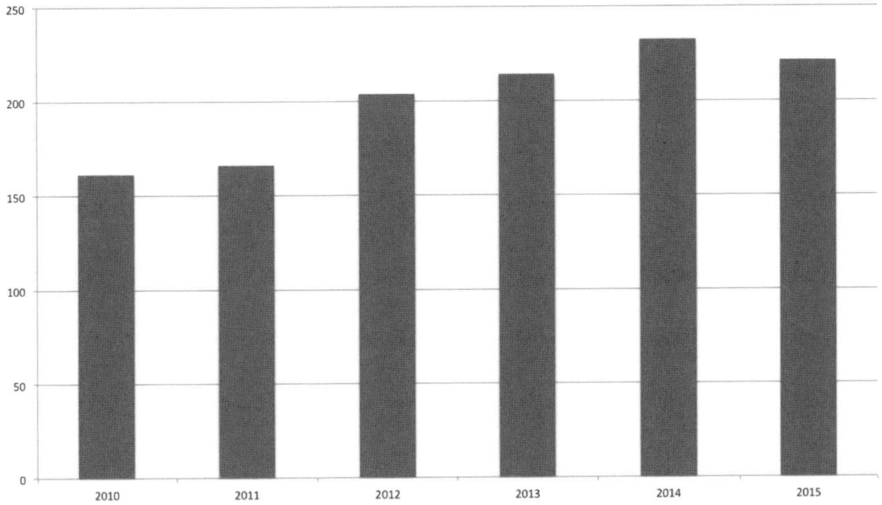

Now we have identified that Domino's has hidden debts in the form of operating leases, the next step is to evaluate the additional risk these commitments add.

How to analyse a company with large rental agreements

When you identify that a company has big future rent commitments, you need to make sure that you don't let these rents confuse you and make you think that a company is better or safer than it really is. Two useful things that you can do are:

1. *Calculate a company's fixed charge cover.* This looks at how many times a company's trading profits can pay the interest payments on borrowings and any rental expenses.

2. *Calculate the capitalised value of operating leases.* This will give you an estimate of hidden debt which you can then use to get a more meaningful estimate of financial risks and ROCE.

1. Fixed charge cover

To calculate the fixed charge cover ratio, you take a company's EBIT or operating profit and add the annual rental expense to it. You do this because EBIT is stated after rental expenses have been already deducted. You want to know the money available to pay rents and interest, so you have to add the rental expense back to EBIT. Once you have this number, you divide it by the rental and interest expenses. Fixed charge cover is calculated as follows:

fixed charge cover =
(EBIT + operating lease expense)/(net interest + operating lease)

For the year to December 2015, Domino's had normalised EBIT of £73.6m, rental expenses of £21.3m and normalised net interest expenses of £0.02m. Its fixed charge cover was therefore:

(73.6 + 21.3)/(0.02 + 21.3) = 4.5 times

This is a healthy figure. It is not uncommon for retailers who rent their stores to have numbers much lower than this. A result within the range of 1.5 to 2 is not unusual. Fixed charge cover of 1.3 times is the lowest level investors should tolerate, as the risk of financial distress becomes significant below that level.

Fixed charge cover has been a great way to spot retailers in trouble in the past, such as HMV, Game Group and Woolworths. These companies did not have huge amounts of debt on their balance sheets, but the rental commitments crippled them when profits started falling.

The situation at Woolworths is shown in Table 7.2. Even in 2005, Woolworths' fixed charge cover was only 1.3 times which was right at the limit of what is normally comfortable. Once profits started to fall in the following year, the company was in the danger zone. By 2007, the company's finances were close to breaking point. It should not have been a surprise when it filed for bankruptcy in January 2009. Prudent investors would not have invested even in 2005.

Table 7.2: Woolworths' low levels of fixed charge cover (2005–2008)

Woolworths plc (£m)	2005	2006	2007	2008
EBIT	66.0	53.1	18.0	36.6
Net interest	−10.1	−9.4	−10.7	−21.7
Pre-tax profit	55.9	43.7	7.3	14.9
Total borrowings	99.7	160.4	131.7	162.9
Operating lease expense	171.3	164.0	171.0	163.2
Fixed charge cover(x)	1.3	1.3	1.0	1.1

By contrast, Domino's long-term figures for fixed charge cover – as shown in Figure 7.2 – shouldn't give investors any cause for concern.

Figure 7.2: Domino's fixed charge cover, 2007–2015

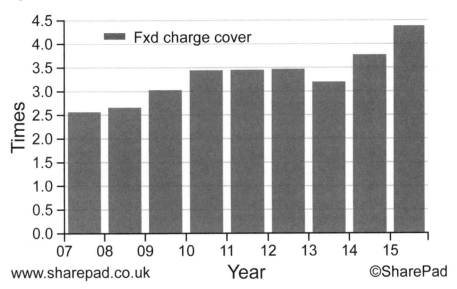

Figure 7.2 shows that Domino's fixed charge cover has been consistently healthy despite the rapid growth in new stores. As the profitability of new stores increases, the fixed charge cover should improve.

Domino's is somewhat unusual because it is a franchising business. It sublets the buildings it is renting out to its franchisees: the franchisee commits to pay the rent. This gives it an extra level of protection and explains why its fixed charge cover is not a matter for concern.

2. Capitalising the value of operating leases

There are two ways to estimate the value of hidden debt by taking an approach that is referred to as capitalising operating leases. In other words, you are working out what the total amount of the future liability might be in today's money.

1. The first way is to discount the future lease commitments to their present value using an interest rate similar to the interest rate paid on existing borrowings.

2. A quicker way, used by the credit rating agencies, is to multiply the current annual rental expense by a multiple between 6 and 8. This is the approach that I use as it is simpler and much more straightforward.

Table 7.3 shows an estimate of hidden debt or capitalised operating leases for Domino's, derived by discounting future leases at an interest rate of 6% (the first of the two methods).

Table 7.3: Domino's hidden debt, estimated by discounting future leases at 6%

Minimum leases 2015	Amount	DF @ 6%	Present value
Year 1	20,380	0.943	19,226
Year 2	17,989	0.890	16,010
Year 3	17,989	0.840	15,104
Year 4	17,989	0.792	14,249
Year 5	17,989	0.747	13,442
After 5 years (av. 10 years)	128,865	0.558	71,958
Total	**221,201**		**149,989**

Minimum leases 2014	Amount	DF @ 6%	Present value
Year 1	19,696	0.943	18,581
Year 2	18,015	0.890	16,033
Year 3	18,015	0.840	15,126
Year 4	18,015	0.792	14,270
Year 5	18,015	0.747	13,462
After 5 years (av. 10 years)	140,770	0.558	78,605
Total	**232,526**		**156,077**

I am using the future operating lease commitments from Domino's annual accounts shown in Table 7.1. For years two to five, I've taken the total number for 'After one year but not more than five years' and divided by four to get an estimate for each individual year (for 2015 this was £71.954m/4 = £17.989m). The amount outstanding after five years has been discounted back to a present value with the estimate that the average number of outstanding leases is 10 years.

To work out a present value you multiply the rent payment for each year by something known as a discount factor (DF). This reduces a future value of something to a present value. The bigger the interest rate, the bigger the discount factor and the lower the present value.

You can work out present values easily using a simple scientific calculator or a spreadsheet. The discount factor to apply to each year's rent payment is based on the following formula:

$$1/(1+i)^n$$

Where i is the rate of interest and n refers to the number of years.

For Domino's in 2015 we would use the following discount factors at an interest rate of 6%:

- Year 1 = 1/1.06 = 0.9434

- Year 2 = 1/1.06^2 = 0.8900

- Year 3 = 1/1.06^3 = 0.8396

- Year 4 = 1/1.06^4 = 0.7921

- Year 5 = 1/1.06^5 = 0.747

If you are using a spreadsheet you calculate a two-year discount factor at 6% by typing =1/1.06^2.

We know that the value of £20.38m in one year's time at an interest rate of 6% has a present value of £19.27m. To help your understanding, you can also say that the future value in one year's time of £19.27m invested at an interest rate of 6% is £20.38m.

This approach reveals that Domino's hidden debt could be around £150m, down from £156m in 2014.

To use the simpler method of multiplying by a number between six and eight, you find a company's annual rental expense by looking at the notes to the annual accounts. It will be labelled 'operating lease payments', or something similar. For 2015, the lease or rent expenses for Domino's was £21,313m, which can be seen in Table 7.4. If we multiply that by 8, we get £170.5m. Thus we can see the estimate is higher using the *8 times annual rental expenses* approach.

Table 7.4: Domino's operating lease payments (December 2015)

	27 Dec 2015 £000	28 Dec 2014 £000
Depreciation of property, plant and equipment	3,427	2,832
Amortisation of prepaid lease charges	196	198
Amortisation of intangible assets	3,156	2,794
Total depreciation and amortisation expense	6,779	5,824
Operating lease payments (minimum lease payments)	21,313	20,874
Impairment loss/(reversal) recognised on non-current assets	326	1,036
Net foreign currency (gain)/loss	[177]	102
Cost of inventories recognised as an expense	139,870	132,085

In Table 7.5, I have shown the range of results derived by multiplying the 2014 and 2015 figures (shown in the column 'Total' and the row 'Total operating lease payments recognised in the income statement' in Table 7.4) by 6, 7 and 8 respectively.

Table 7.5: Domino's estimated capitalised value of operating leases

£m	2015	2014
Rent expense	21.313	20.874
Capitalised at 8x	170.5	167.0
Capitalised at 7x	149.2	146.1
Capitalised at 6x	127.9	125.2

Figure 7.3 shows how the amount of Domino's hidden debts has evolved over the years. As you can see, they have been growing as the company has opened up more Pizza shops.

Figure 7.3: Domino's increasing hidden debts (2006–2015)

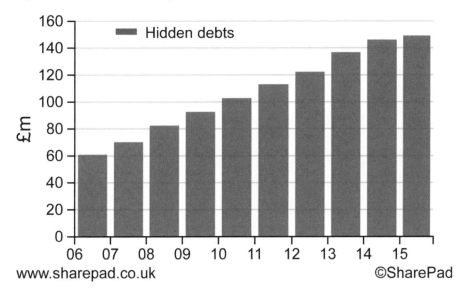

These calculations are all well and good, but how are they useful to an investor?

The impact on ROCE

In Part 1, I showed you how to calculate a company's lease-adjusted ROCE, which takes into account its hidden debts. You can use the same method to check whether hidden debts make a company a risky investment. This gives you a truer picture of a company's financial performance. In most cases, ROCE will decline when hidden debts are included.

Table 7.6 shows the ROCE and lease-adjusted ROCE for a selection of retailing companies to illustrate how big this difference can be.

Table 7.6: ROCE and lease-adjusted ROCE figures for retail companies

Company	Capital employed (£m)	Lease-adj. capital employed (£m)	Est. hidden debt (£m)	ROCE (%)	Lease-adj. ROCE (%)
Next	1501.9	3004.1	1502.2	60.2	33.2
JD Sports Fashion	449.4	1372.7	923.3	37.4	16.8
WH Smith	188.0	1987.0	1799.0	69.4	12.9

Company	Capital employed (£m)	Lease-adj. capital employed (£m)	Est. hidden debt (£m)	ROCE (%)	Lease-adj. ROCE (%)
Sports Direct Int.	1392.3	2395.5	1003.2	21.9	15.9
Dunelm Group	241.5	514.0	272.5	51.6	28.8
Home Retail Group	1986.4	3156.1	1169.7	1.7	3.4
Card Factory	411.3	666.1	254.8	20.7	15.8
Darty	204.1	759.3	555.2	19.4	10.5
Halfords Group	505.4	1152.2	646.8	17.0	11.3

Source: Figures sourced from 2015/16 annual reports

Many retailers rent rather than own their high street stores, which means they have a lot of hidden debts. Without taking these debts into account these companies can look like very good businesses with very high ROCEs. Once the debts are factored in, this changes. Next still looks good, for example, but WH Smith sees a big fall in ROCE.

There's nothing wrong with investing in companies with hidden debts, but it makes sense to ensure that they pass the tests of quality and safety. By this I mean:

- A minimum adjusted ROCE of 15%.

- A minimum fixed charge cover of at least 2.

Be wary of sale and leasebacks

In recent times, one of the easiest ways for companies to raise cash has been to sell some of their properties to property companies or investment funds and then rent them back. This is known as a sale and leaseback transaction. For supermarket companies such as Tesco, this was a big warning sign that all was not well.

Without the cash proceeds from selling supermarket stores to property companies, Tesco would have been struggling to find the free cash flow to pay dividends or invest in its business. The cash inflow from property sales made it look as if Tesco's debt was nothing to worry about, but the off-balance-sheet debt increased at a rapid rate from 2005 to 2013 (as shown in Figure 7.4).

After selling a number of its stores, Tesco tied itself into long-term rent agreements for stores that aren't as profitable as they used to be. This was one of the main reasons why Tesco had to stop paying a dividend in 2015. Trying to get out of these rented stores could prove to be very expensive for Tesco in the future. This is a good example of why investors ignore hidden debt at their peril.

Figure 7.4: Tesco's future rent obligations (2005–2015)

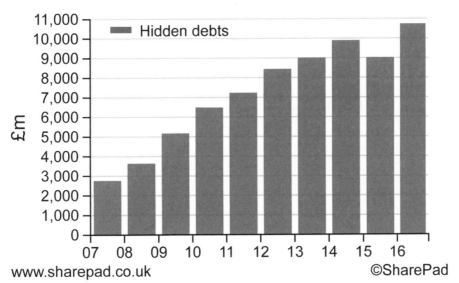

We have seen that hidden debts can be significant liabilities and should not be ignored by investors. Now you know what to look for and how to analyse hidden debts you can keep yourself away from companies where the risks posed by them are too high.

As well as hidden debts, one of the biggest risks facing shareholders comes from investing in companies with big pension fund deficits. This is the subject of the next chapter.

8

THE DANGERS OF PENSION FUND DEFICITS

P ENSIONS ARE SOMETIMES regarded as a pretty dry subject. Nevertheless, they are a very important consideration for investors.

You should always remember that a shareholder is only entitled to the profits and cash flows of a company after all expenses and liabilities have been paid. The more liabilities that are in front of investors, the less money they are entitled to and the more risky an investment in the company will be. A company's pension scheme is one of the liabilities it is faced with and which must be paid before shareholders.

Due to a variety of reasons, lots of corporate pension funds have significant funding shortfalls, known as deficits. This means that the assets within the pension fund are not sufficient to pay all the future pensions the company has promised to its past and current employees. When this happens, the company has to find the cash to pay pensions from somewhere else, which will limit the cash that is free to distribute to shareholders. An important message of this chapter is that you should avoid investing in companies with large pension fund deficits.

At the end of the chapter, you will understand the big impact pension fund deficits can have on company profits and cash flows, the amount of dividends shareholders receive, and the implications for the value of a company's shares.

Types of corporate pension schemes

There are two main types of corporate pension scheme:

1. Defined contribution or money purchase schemes.

2. Defined benefit or final salary schemes.

8. THE DANGERS OF PENSION FUND DEFICITS

1. Defined contribution or money purchase pension schemes

Many companies offer defined contribution pension schemes to their employees.

This is where the amount of money paid into the fund by the company is known (it is defined). It is usually a percentage of the employee's salary. This is a known cash cost for the company every year. The amount paid into the pension scheme reduces a company's profits and cash flow, and is an extra cost for the business.

The amount of pension the employee ultimately receives depends on the amount that they and their employer contribute, and the investment returns on the money invested. The company has no further pension obligations to its employees. Companies like this type of pension scheme because once they have paid the pension contributions, they don't have any further pension costs to worry about.

Domino's is an example of a company that has a defined contribution pension scheme for its employees. Its shareholders therefore do not face risks or uncertainty regarding Domino's pension obligations. This is a good position as far as investors are concerned.

2. Defined benefit or final salary schemes

These pension funds are more problematic for companies.

Here, the benefit – the employee's pension – is defined. It is usually based on a percentage of the employee's final salary.

The problem for the company is that it requires enough money to pay the employees' pensions for the rest of their lives when they have retired. This can end up being a very large sum of money and it is not an easy number to work out. Companies employ actuaries to make these calculations for them.

These pension funds can become a big problem for companies when the amount of money they have set aside (pension fund assets) is less than the amount they will have to pay out in future pensions (pension fund liabilities). Under these circumstances, the pension fund is said to have a deficit and the company has to find the money needed to make up the shortfall.

When the deficit is large, a company may have to cut its dividend payments to shareholders. In extreme cases, the deficit may bankrupt the company.

This is the reason why most final salary schemes have been closed to new members and the benefits have been cut for existing members. Companies have realised that commitments to pay defined benefit pensions are too expensive. For example, BT's final salary scheme was closed to new members in 2001, although it still remains a big problem for the company today.

Let's look at the BT situation as an illustrative case study.

BT's final salary pension scheme

At the end of March 2015, BT's final salary pension fund had a deficit of £7.6bn, as shown in Table 8.1. This was because the value of the fund was £43.6bn, but the present value of its future pension liabilities was £51.2bn. The deficit is shown on the company's balance sheet as a liability and thus it reduces the amount of shareholders' equity.

Table 8.1: BT balance sheet, £m (March 2015)

	2015	2014
Non-current assets		
Intangible assets	3,170	3,087
Property, plant and equipment	13,505	13,840
Derivative financial instruments	1,232	539
Investments	44	34
Associates and joint ventures	26	18
Trade and other receivables	184	214
Deferred tax assets	1,559	1,460
	19,720	19,192
Current assets		
Programme rights	118	108
Inventories	94	82
Trade and other receivables	3,140	2,907
Current tax receivable	65	26
Derivative financial instruments	97	114
Investments	3,523	1,774
Cash and cash equivalents	434	695
	7,471	5,706
Current liabilities		
Loans and other borrowings	1,900	1,873
Derivative financial instruments	168	139
Trade and other payables	5,276	5,261
Current tax liabilities	222	315
Provisions	142	99
	7,708	7,687
Total assets less current liabilities	**19,483**	**17,211**

	2015	2014
Non-current liabilities		
Loans and other borrowings	7,868	7,941
Derivative financial instruments	927	679
Retirement benefit obligations	7,583	7,022
Other payables	927	898
Deferred tax liabilities	948	829
Provisions	422	434
	18,675	17,803
Equity		
Ordinary shares	419	408
Share premium	1,051	62
Own shares	[165]	[829]
Other reserves	1,485	1,447
Retained loss	[1,982]	[1,680]
Total equity (deficit)	**808**	**[592]**
	19,483	17,211

The net pension deficit (or obligation) is shown as being £6.1bn. The £7.6bn deficit had been reduced by a deferred tax asset of £1.5bn. (To see the net pension deficit you have to go and look into the notes of the company's accounts. There will be a number next to the pension deficit figure on the balance sheet that will tell you where to look.) This asset exists because if the company wanted to get rid of its deficit in full today, it would have to make £7.6bn of payments into the fund and it would get tax relief of £1.5bn on those payments. This is all shown in Table 8.1.

But how does a fund end up in deficit in the first place?

Let's take a look at how its assets and liabilities are comprised.

Table 8.2 shows a section from BT's 2015 annual report. It shows how the assets and the liabilities of a final salary pension scheme are made up and how they change during a year.

Table 8.2: BT retirement benefit plan assets and liabilities (2015)

	Assets (£m)	Liabilities (£m)	Deficit (£m)
At 1 April 2013	41,566	[47,422]	[5,856]
Current service cost	-	[272]	[272]
Interest on pension deficit	1,710	[1,945]	[235]
Settlements	[63]	61	[2]
Administration expenses and Pension Protection Fund (PPF) levy	[40]	-	[40]
Included in the group income statement	**1,607**	**[2,156]**	**[549]**
Return on plan assets below the amount included in the group income statement	[1,453]	-	[1,453]
Actuarial gain arising from changes in financial assumptions	-	580	580
Actuarial loss arising from changes in demographic assumptions	-	-	-
Actuarial loss arising from experience adjustments	-	[306]	[306]
Included in the group statement of comprehensive income	**[1,453]**	**274**	**[1,179]**
Regular contributions by employer	228	-	228
Deficit contributions by employer	325	-	325
Included in the group cash flow statement	**553**	**-**	**553**
Contributions by employees	12	[12]	-
Benefits paid 2013/14	[2,166]	2,166	-
Foreign exchange	[6]	15	9
Other movements	**[2,160]**	**2,169**	**9**
At 31 March 2014	40,113	[47,135]	[7,022]
Current service cost	-	[254]	[254]
Interest on pension deficit	1,663	[1,955]	[292]
Past service credit	-	5	5
Administration expenses and PPF levy	[42]	-	[42]
Included in the group income statement	**1,621**	**[2,204]**	**[583]**
Return on plan assets above the amount included in the group income statement	3,083	-	3,083
Actuarial loss arising from changes in financial assumptions	-	[4,703]	[4,703]
Actuarial gain arising from changes in demographic assumptions	-	126	126

	Assets (£m)	Liabilities (£m)	Deficit (£m)
Actuarial gain arising from experience adjustments	-	443	443
Included in the group statement of comprehensive income	**3,083**	**[4,134]**	**[1,051]**
Regular contributions by employer	178	-	178
Deficit contributions by employer	876	-	876
Included in the group cash flow statement	**1,054**	**-**	**1,054**
Contributions by employees	12	[12]	-
Benefits paid 2014/15	[2,231]	2,231	-
Foreign exchange	[25]	44	19
Other movements	**[2,244]**	**2,263**	**19**
At 31 March 2015	43,627	[51,210]	[7,583]

Let's start by looking at the assets first.

Pension fund assets

The assets of the pension fund are made up of the value of different investments such as shares, bonds, property and cash. The value of these investments has to be shown at fair value. This is often the market value for investments such as shares and bonds. If there isn't a market valuation available, the actuary will estimate a value. At the end of March 2014, the value of the fund's assets was £40.1bn.

The actuary then estimates the annual investment return (price changes plus any income received such as dividends) on those assets. This was expected to be £1663m for the year to March 2015. This £1663m divided by the starting asset value of £40,113 tells us that the estimated return was 4.14% – a similar assumption to the 4.11% in 2014. This return is added to the fund's asset value and is also treated as interest income in BT's income statement (more later on this).

An administrative expense of £42m was paid. This reduces the asset value.

There is then an addition of £3083m. This represents an extra amount of money earned from investment returns above the amount assumed by the actuary (£1663m). This tells us that the fund produced total investment returns of £4746m (£3083m + £1663m) during the year.

Then we have the amount of £1054m that BT paid into the fund. This is made up of regular contributions of £178m and top up payments of £876m to reduce the deficit. This is a cash outflow for BT, and a large one at that. This is an important number for investors to pay attention to as it has the biggest impact on the company's free cash and thus on dividends.

Next come the contributions of £12m paid by employees, which adds to assets.

The biggest reduction in assets comes from the amount of money actually used to pay pensions, which was £2244m. After this has been paid, the fund ends the year with assets of £43.6bn, or £2.5bn more than it started with.

This is encouraging, but is only half the story. You have to take into account what has happened to the liabilities as well.

Pension fund liabilities

As well as looking at the size of the pension fund deficit, you should also focus on the size of the liability to pay future pensions. This is what is going to have the biggest impact on cash flowing out of the business in the future and therefore how much cash flow will be free to distribute to shareholders.

These liabilities are the present value of all the future payments that have to be made to current and future pensioners. How this number is arrived at involves some very complicated calculations which are worked out by an actuary. At the end of 2014, the value of these liabilities for BT was £47.1bn.

In order to work out the value of the liability, the actuary uses the following variables:

1. The rate of increases in workers' salaries between now and their retirement date.

2. When the workers will retire.

3. What proportion of their final salary they will be paid.

4. How long they will live after they retire. In other words, how long the company will have to pay the pension for.

5. The rate of inflation in the future as pension payments are often linked to inflation.

A liability will be worked out for each worker and then all the liabilities will be added together. The value of this liability then has to be discounted to a present value at the balance sheet date.

The discount rate is based on the yield of good quality bonds (which is open to interpretation). The lower the yield on those bonds, the higher the present value of the liability. Many pension fund liabilities have been rising in recent years due to lower interest rates on bonds and the assumption that pensioners are living longer.

As I've just said, working out pension fund liabilities is a complicated task. However, a very simple way of understanding the impact of interest rates on these liabilities is to consider the following example. It's not how liabilities are worked out in practice, but it will help you understand them.

Say an employee's pension based on their final salary is £10,000 per year. If interest rates on government bonds are 10% then the employer would need £100,000 to produce that income (£100,000 x 10%). If interest rates fall to 5%, the employer would then need £200,000 to produce £10,000 per year (£20,000 x 5%). So falling interest rates are bad news for companies with final salary pension schemes.

If interest rates on bonds decrease in the future then some companies will have to put more cash into their pension funds. This could mean that there is less cash spare to pay dividends to shareholders. On the other hand, if bond rates rise enough these deficits will shrink or even disappear.

Let's look at BT's pension fund liabilities again and see how they change from year to year.

Starting with a value of £47.1bn, a current service cost of £254m is added to the liability. This is the amount of future pension benefit that current employees have earned during the year.

Then an interest expense is added to the liability. This interest charge is also treated as an expense in the income statement. The £1955m of interest expense is effectively the unwinding of part of the total present value of liabilities. It occurs because part of the liability has become closer to being paid.

We then see a big addition to the liability of £4.1bn due to changes in assumptions versus those assumed by the actuary. BT explains the reasons for this change in a footnote.

The other big number is the £2231m paid out to pensioners. This reduces the liability because it has been paid and doesn't need to be paid again.

Overall, the value of liabilities ended the year more than £4bn higher than when it started and led to the size of the deficit increasing.

Final salary pension schemes and profits

The pension fund surplus or deficit is shown on a company's balance sheet. The costs associated with final salary pension schemes are treated as expenses in a company's income statement. Table 8.3 shows part of BT's income statement for March 2015.

Table 8.3: BT's income statement, £m (March 2015)

	2015	2014	2013
Recognised in the income statement before specific items			
Current service cost:			
– defined benefit plans	254	272	225
– defined contribution plans	176	151	136
Past service credit	[5]	-	-
Administration expenses and Pension Protection Fund (PPF) levy	42	40	38
Total operating expense	467	463	399
Net interest expense on net pensions deficit included in specific items	292	235	117
Total recognised in the income statement	759	698	516

BT has charged £254m of current service cost and £292m of interest (£1663m of assumed investment returns less £1955 on interest on pension fund liabilities) as an expense in its income statement. The interest part of it has been included in specific items and was not used to calculate the company's underlying profits. Not all companies follow this approach and it could be seen to be slightly aggressive accounting by BT.

On the other hand, you could argue that these amounts of interest income and expense are not real cash flows and it is quite right to exclude them.

Impact on cash flows

What the company actually pays into the final salary pension scheme is much more important than what is expensed in the income statement. This is what affects the company's annual free cash flows and its ability to pay dividends to shareholders. Table 8.4 shows the payments made by BT into its pension scheme for March 2015.

Table 8.4: BT's pension costs in the cash flow statement

Year ended 31 March (£m)	2015	2014
Ordinary contributions	168	205
Deficit contributions	875	325
Total contributions in the year	1,043	530

8. THE DANGERS OF PENSION FUND DEFICITS

Notes from the accounts

The group made a deficit contribution payment of £625m in April 2015 and expects to make further contributions of approximately £510m to the BTPS in 2015/16, comprising ordinary contributions of approximately £260m and deficit contributions of £250m.

Future funding obligations and recovery plan

Under the terms of the Trust Deed, the group is required to have a funding plan, determined at the triennial of the funding valuation, which is a legal agreement between BT and the Trustee and should address the deficit over a maximum period of 20 years.

In January 2015, the 2014 triennial funding valuation was finalised, agreed with the Trustee and certified by the Scheme Actuary. The funding deficit at 30 June 2014 was £7.0bn. Under the associated recovery plan BT made payments of £8.75m in March 2015 and £625m in April 2015. BT will make future deficit payments in line with the table below.

Future funding obligations and recovery plan								
Year to 31 March	**2016**	**2017**	**2018**	**2019**	**2020**	**2021**	**2022**	**2023**
Deficit contribution (£m)	250	250	688	699	711	724	670	670
Year to 31 March	**2024**	**2025**	**2026**	**2027**	**2028**	**2029**	**2030**	
Deficit contribution (£m)	670	495	495	495	495	495	289	

Table 8.4 shows that BT paid over £1bn into its final salary pension fund in the previous year. £168m was an ordinary contribution, which was less than its current service charge (the amount of future pension benefit earned by employees during the year of £254m) and £875m was a top-up payment with the aim of reducing the deficit.

In the company's operating cash flow, the excess cash paid over the current service charge expensed in the income statement will be shown as a cash outflow. With £1.043m of cash paid against the £254m of current service charge expensed, the cash outflow would be £789m and would reduce BT's operating cash flow by that amount. This is shown in the £727m decrease in other liabilities in Table 8.5. (The £789m cash outflow from the pension contribution is being bundled up with other cash flows here.)

As you can see in the notes in Table 8.4, BT made another top up payment of £625m in April 2015 with another £250m to be made before March 2016. These top-up payments have been agreed with the pension fund trustees and will total £8.7bn between 2015 and 2030. That's £8.7bn that cannot be paid as dividends to shareholders.

Table 8.5: Differences between pension income statement expense and cash paid into pension scheme, £m

Group cash flow statement	2015	2014	2013
Cash flow from operating activities			
Profit before taxation	2,645	2,312	2,315
(Profit) loss on disposal of interest in associates and joint ventures	[25]	4	[130]
Share of post tax loss (profit) of associates and joint ventures	1	3	[9]
Net finance expense	859	826	772
Operating profit	3,480	3,145	2,948
Other non-cash charges	[19]	39	56
Loss (profit) on disposal of businesses	1	-	[7]
Depreciation and amortisation	2,538	2,695	2,843
(Increase) decrease in inventories	[13]	16	3
(Increase) decrease in trade and other receivables	[137]	[259]	454
Decrease in trade and other payables	[37]	[159]	[459]
Decrease in other liabilities	[727]	[234]	[281]
Increase (decrease) in provisions	19	[100]	[198]
Cash generated from operations	**5,105**	**5,143**	**5,359**
Income taxes paid	[309]	[347]	[64]
Net cash inflow from operating activities	**4,796**	**4,796**	**5,295**

Implications for dividend payments

Despite the large amount of pension deficit payments that are being paid, BT has still been producing enough free cash flow to comfortably cover its dividend payments, as shown in Figure 8.1. This is not always the case with other companies with pension fund deficits and this is something you need to watch out for.

Figure 8.1: BT's free cash flow per share (FCFps) and adjusted dividends per share (DPS) (2007–2016)

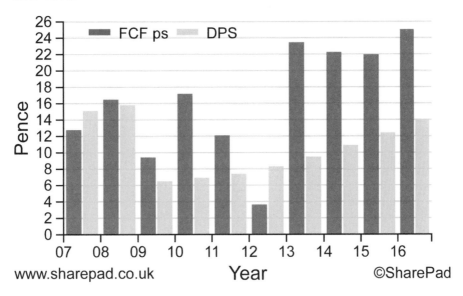

www.sharepad.co.uk   Year   ©SharePad

Identifying big pension fund deficits

One of the ways to see if a company has a big – and potentially problematic – pension fund deficit is to compare it with the market value of its equity, as represented by its market capitalisation.

To do this, you just divide the size of the pension fund deficit found on a company's balance sheet by the market capitalisation of the company. You work out a company's market capitalisation by multiplying the number of shares in issue by the current share price. This information is freely available on the internet for listed companies.

Table 8.6 shows a range of companies with large pension fund deficits as at December 2016.

As you can see, there are some companies with big pension fund black holes out there. Trinity Mirror, for example, has a pension fund deficit of 129% of its market capitalisation. When you find a company with a large pension deficit, you need to take great care before buying its shares, even if it has other high-quality characteristics such as a high ROCE and strong free cash flow.

Personally, I would avoid companies with pension fund deficits that are any more than 10% of market capitalisation.

Table 8.6: Corporate pension fund deficits, December 2016

Name	Pension deficit (£m)	Market cap. (£m)	Pension deficit % of market cap.
Trinity Mirror	−305.2	236.1	−129.0%
Hogg Robinson Group	−258.3	205.9	−125%
Renold	−82.8	99.2	−83.5%
Communisis	−41.1	75.4	−54.6%
Norcros	−55.7	110.3	−50.5%
Mothercare	−74.4	188.8	−39.4%
De La Rue	−219.9	588.4	−37.4%
Carillion	−393.5	1058.9	−37.2%
Wincanton	−105.6	285.9	−36.9%
Thomas Cook Group	−449.0	1384.6	−32.4%
Mitchells & Butlers	−291.0	960.1	−30.3%
GKN	−1594.0	5458.9	−29.2%
Carclo	−23.2	90.5	−25.6%
Morgan Advanced Materials	−204.5	825.6	−24.8%
Charles Taylor	−39.6	166.4	−23.8%
BAE Systems	−4501.0	19197.3	−23.4%
FirstGroup	−270.9	1230.5	−22.0%
Devro	−56.4	261.7	−21.6%

Pension fund deficits and the investor

Should you avoid buying the shares of companies with pension fund deficits?

If you want to minimise your investment risks then it is probably a good idea to avoid companies with pension fund deficits. That said, there are a number of checks that you can do to work out if a pension fund deficit is exposing you to big risks:

1. Does the company have enough free cash flow to plug the hole in its pension fund and still have enough money leftover to pay dividends? Check out the company's free cash flow dividend cover.

2. Take the size of the deficit and divide it by ten. Most pension fund deficits have to be closed over ten years. This calculation will tell you how much extra

cash the company needs to pay into the fund. So for BT, with a £7bn shortfall it should be paying in an extra £700m a year for the next ten years. Is the company paying enough? BT looks like it is, having paid £875m last year. Other companies might not be.

3. If a company looks like it isn't paying enough to reduce the deficit, work out how much the extra payments would reduce a company's free cash flow and then compare that with the cash cost of the company's dividend. Can the company still afford to pay the dividend?

4. Look at the sensitivities of the pension fund to changes in assumptions about interest rates, future inflation and life expectancy of pensioners in retirement. These can have a big impact on the value of the pension fund liability and the future cash flows required to plug the gap, as shown for BT in Table 8.7. This table is showing you how sensitive BT's pension liability and deficit are to changes to key measures such as discount rates, expected inflation and the life expectancy of the scheme members. For example, if members are assumed to live one year longer than they are currently, the deficit will increase by £1bn. That means £1bn off the value of the company's equity, which means a lower share price. This is why avoiding companies with big pension fund deficits is probably a good idea.

Table 8.7: BT Final salary pension fund sensitivities

	Decrease (increase) in liability (£bn)	Decrease (increase) in deficit (£bn)
0.25 percentage point increase to:		
– discount rate	1.9	1.2
– inflation rate (assuming RPI, CPI and salary increases all move by 0.25 percentage points	[1.5]	[0.5]
– CPI inflation rate (assuming RPI and salary increases are unchanged)	[1]	[1]
– salary increases (assuming RPI and CPI are unchanged)	[0.2]	[0.2]
Additional one year increase to life expectancy	[1.3]	[1]

PART 2 SUMMARY

HOW TO AVOID DANGEROUS COMPANIES

I N THIS SECTION we have looked at what makes a company dangerous and how you can avoid these investments. The first step in avoiding them is to invest in high-quality businesses, which we talked about in part one.

Apart from poor-quality companies, investors should avoid companies with lots of debt and debt-like liabilities. In my opinion, the ideal company to invest in is one with as little debt as possible. That said, a prudent amount of debt could be helpful. In order to stay away from companies where debt could be a problem, I find it useful to stick to these rules:

1. Debt to net operating cash flow of less than 3 times.

2. Debt to free cash flow of less than 10 times.

3. Debt to total assets of less than 50%.

4. Interest cover more than 5 times.

5. Fixed charge cover more than 2 times.

And I would take a long hard look at these:

1. Pension fund deficit less than 10% of market capitalisation.

2. Interest rates on debts fixed rather than floating.

3. Avoid large amounts of debt repayable in one year or less.

PART 3

HOW TO VALUE A COMPANY'S SHARES

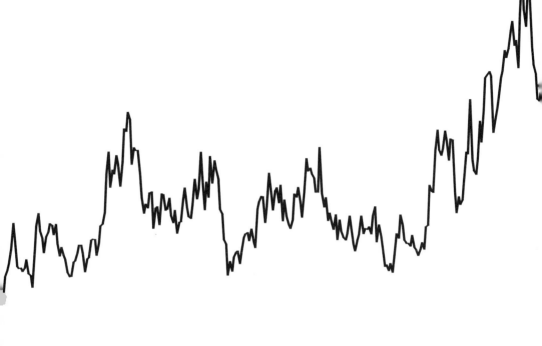

PART 3 – HOW TO VALUE A COMPANY'S SHARES

YOU NOW KNOW how to discover a high-quality company that doesn't have too much debt. It has passed the quality and safety tests that you should be looking for in winning shares.

So why not go straight ahead and buy?

Because quality and safety alone are not enough to produce winning investments. You have to pay the right price for them. Like many good things in life, more often than not you have to pay for quality. You are very unlikely to be able buy a sensational bottle of wine for £5, or a Ferrari for the price of a Ford. But you mustn't pay too much.

Paying too much for a great company is the biggest mistake that investors make. They fall in love with how good the company is and think that its shares are a buy at any price. They are not. Overpaying for shares is a way to lose money.

However, you must also not be frightened of paying a reasonably high valuation for a high-quality business. The biggest lesson I've learned in nearly 20 years of investing is that you can rarely expect to buy high-quality businesses at bargain basement prices. My reluctance to pay up for quality has seen me lose out on many potentially profitable investments in the past.

In Part 3, I look at how to value the shares of a company so that you can be confident that you are paying a reasonable price and not paying too much.

I begin by looking at the basics of share valuations and what they are actually telling you. Following the basics, I move on to how you should actually value a share. I look at how to calculate a company's cash profits and then use them to value a share. I show how to work out how much of a company's share price is based on its current profits and how much of the price is based on growing profits in the future. Finally, I show how to calculate the maximum price you should pay for a share.

9

THE BASICS OF SHARE VALUATION

YOU CAN ONLY make money from investing in shares of good-quality companies if you pay the right price for the shares. A common mistake by investors is to think that buying quality companies is all that matters, and the price paid for the shares is irrelevant. This is not the case.

Paying too high a price for a share is one of the biggest risks that you can take as an investor. It is just as bad as investing in a poor-quality company in the first place. The key to successful long-term investing is buying good companies at good prices.

In this chapter, we look at why valuation – the price of a share – is crucial to your long-term investing success. You will learn how to value the shares of companies and set target prices for buying and selling them.

The valuation of shares can become a very complicated exercise. There are lots of books out there on this subject and many make the process seem difficult to understand. The good news is that it doesn't have to be this way. Valuing shares is not a precise science: you only need to be roughly right and err on the side of caution.

The place to start is looking at the fair value of a share.

The fair value of a share

Professional analysts and investors spend lots of time trying to work out how much a share of a company is really worth. To do this they need to estimate how much free cash flow the company will produce for its shareholders for the rest of its life and put a value on that in today's money, which is known as a present value. This approach is known as a discounted cash flow (DCF) valuation. It is exactly the same process that was used to estimate the value of hidden debts in Chapter 7.

It is impossible to predict the future with complete accuracy one year in advance, never mind decades into the future, and you shouldn't even try to do this. It's just not worth spending a lot of time on this. You are going to be wrong.

However, if you take a little bit of time to understand how share valuations are arrived at you will begin to understand why they are so important and why paying too much for a share is a bad thing to do.

Let's look at the valuation of Domino's Pizza shares in July 2016 using a DCF approach when the shares were priced at 320p each. There are three steps to doing a DCF valuation:

1. *Estimate free cash flow per share for a period of future years.* Most analysts would probably try to forecast ten years of future free cash flows. I've assumed that Domino's can grow at 10% a year for five years and that growth rate declines 1% a year from then on, to reach 5% at the end of year ten.

2. *Choose what interest rate you want to receive in order to invest in the shares.* This subject is worthy of a book in itself and there is no definitive answer to what is the right rate. The simple answer is that shares are risky investments – more risky than savings accounts and most bonds – and so people demand to receive a higher interest rate in order to invest in them. To keep the numbers simple, I've chosen an interest rate, or discount rate, of 10% to discount these future cash flows back to a present value.

3. *Estimate what the value of the shares might be in ten years' time and give that a value in today's money.* This is known as a terminal value and it stops you having to estimate free cash flows forever. You estimate it by taking a long-run, steady-state growth estimate in free cash flows and get a value using the following formula: terminal value = year 11 FCF/(interest rate – long-term growth rate).

For Domino's, I've assumed that after year 10, free cash flows grow at 5% forever which gives an estimate of the share price in ten years' time of 588p (28 × 1.05/ (10% – 5%)).

Table 9.1 shows these three steps in action. In the FCFps column, I have listed the future free cash flows for each year based upon my expectations of 10% growth to year five, then a 1% fall in growth for five years after that. So, for example, the free cash flows in year 2 are a 10% increase on 13.6p, which is 15p (14.96p). In year 6, the cash flows are a 9% increase on the cash flows of year 5, which is 21.8p.

In the discount factor column, I have shown what number you have to multiply the forecast free cash flow by to get a present value at an interest rate of 10%.

In the present value column, you see what the present value of future free cash flow is at an interest rate of 10%. The lower the interest/discount rate you use, the higher the present value is and vice versa.

The estimated value of the shares is then arrived at by summing the total of the present values of the future cash flows per share and adding this to the present value of the terminal value of the shares (226.7p), which gives a result of 346.9p.

Table 9.1: Domino's Pizza discounted cash flow (DCF) valuation, 10% interest rate

Forecast year	FCFps (p)	Growth rate	Discount factor @ 10%	Present value
1	13.6	10%	0.9091	12.4
2	15.0	10%	0.8264	12.4
3	16.5	10%	0.7513	12.4
4	18.2	10%	0.6830	12.4
5	20.0	10%	0.6209	12.4
6	21.8	9%	0.5645	12.3
7	23.5	8%	0.5132	12.1
8	25.2	7%	0.4665	11.8
9	26.7	6%	0.4241	11.3
10	28.0	5%	0.3855	10.8
Terminal value	578.0		0.3855	226.7
Est. value per share (p)				**346.9**

Based on these assumptions, Domino's shares might be slightly cheap (the estimated value is 346.9p, whereas the current price is 320p). Put another way, the current share price is assuming a reasonable rate of growth going forward.

By doing this discounted cash flow exercise you have learned that the July 2016 share price can be pretty much explained by the growth rates assumed in the table above. So you know that Domino's has to grow at these rates to justify a share price only slightly higher than it was in July 2016. You have learned what future growth rates are implied by share prices. This is very valuable information to an investor. You should only try to buy shares when you think that the future growth rates are likely to be higher than the market currently expects.

But what if Domino's can't grow as fast in the future? What if its profits fall? What if 10% is the wrong discount factor?

If I use a discount factor of 8% instead, I get an estimated value of 565p per share and might think Domino's shares are really cheap, which may or may not be the case. This is shown in Table 9.2.

The choice of discount factor is one of the most hotly disputed numbers in finance and there is no right answer as to what is the correct number. Whole books have been written on this subject. As a rule of thumb, the more risky a business is, the higher discount factor you should use. Risk mainly comes in the form of high debts and company size (smaller companies tend to go bankrupt more than big ones do).

If a company looks undervalued when using a higher discount factor and the assumptions of future growth are realistic and reasonable, then you tend to stand a better chance of identifying an undervalued share. By lowering your discount factor to too low a rate to make a share look cheap, you are taking more risks with your money. I'll have more to say on interest rates for different types of company in Chapter 11.

Table 9.2: Domino's Pizza discounted cash flow (DCF) valuation, 8% interest rate

Forecast year	FCFps(p)	Growth rate	Discount factor @ 8%	Present value
1	13.6	10%	0.9259	12.6
2	15.0	10%	0.8573	12.9
3	16.5	10%	0.7938	13.1
4	18.2	10%	0.7350	13.3
5	20.0	10%	0.6806	13.6
6	21.8	9%	0.6302	13.7
7	23.5	8%	0.5835	13.7
8	25.2	7%	0.5403	13.6
9	26.7	6%	0.5002	13.3
10	28.0	5%	0.4632	13.0
Terminal value	933.2	5%	0.4632	432.3
Est. value per share(p)				**565.1**

This exercise helps you understand the two main reasons why share prices go up and down:

1. *Expectations of future profits move up or down.* This is why share prices get hammered when a company announces that profits will fall, or will grow more slowly than expected. This is known as a profits warning.

2. *Interest rates change.* Lower rates tend to push up share prices. Higher interest rates push them down. The interest rates on UK government bonds have been falling since the early 1980s. The continuous downwards trend in interest rates on bonds and savings accounts has meant the interest rates on shares have become more attractive. Many investors have been prepared to accept a lower interest rate to invest in shares and this has pushed up the prices they are prepared to pay for these shares. Whether they are right to do so is another matter.

Many professional investors do not bother going through this kind of exercise. They know they cannot accurately predict the future and that this kind of approach is only as good as the assumptions behind it. In other words, bad or unrealistic assumptions result in bad and worthless valuations.

Instead they use shortcuts based on multiples of a company's profits, cash flows or assets. This is much simpler and less time consuming. It is possible to work out whether a share is cheap or expensive using the methods I explain in the following chapters. Before I get on to that, I want to say a quick word about the PE ratio.

Don't use the PE ratio

The price to earnings ratio (PE) is the most commonly used valuation yardstick by investors. You will find a company's PE ratio on most investment websites and in the financial section of newspapers.

It is very easy to calculate:

PE ratio = share price/earnings per share (EPS)

In simple terms, shares with high PE ratios are seen as being expensive whilst those with low ones are seen as being cheaper. Yet, despite its simplicity, I do not use the PE ratio as I feel it has many pitfalls that can give investors a misleading view of how cheap or expensive some shares really are. The PE ratio's drawbacks are all to do with the 'E', or EPS, part of the calculation:

1. *EPS is easy to manipulate*: Companies can boost EPS by changing accounting policies. For example, they can extend the useful lives of fixed assets such as plant and machinery, which lowers the depreciation expense and boosts profits.

2. *EPS says nothing about the quality of profits:* It doesn't take into account whether profits have changed due to sales of existing products or services – the best source of profits growth – or whether the company has invested heavily in new assets or bought another company. Share buybacks boost EPS by shrinking the number of shares outstanding, even if profits are static or shrinking. Buybacks

151

can be done when the shares are expensive. Let me illustrate what I mean by returning to Bob's Book Store, a fictional business we met in Part 2.

Bob has built up a very successful business over the years. He is making a very impressive £100m of trading profits every year but stiff competition means that this number is unlikely to change much. He has no debt and has £160m of cash sitting in a bank account earning no interest. The stock market is in buoyant mood though and has given his shares a very punchy valuation of £1.6 billion, or 20 times earnings (a PE ratio of 20) despite the low or non-existent growth prospects.

Bob needs to keep his shareholders happy. His advisors suggest buying back 10% of the existing shares in issue (in this case 100 million of them) so that earnings per share (EPS) can keep growing. So instead of paying a dividend Bob decides to use £160m of cash sitting in the bank to buy back shares at the price of 160p each instead.

Bob is pleased with the results. Even with no growth in profits, EPS has increased by 11.1%, as shown Table 9.3.

Table 9.3: Bob's Book Store before and after the share buyback

Bob's Book Store (£m)	Before buyback	After buyback
Trading profit	100	100
Interest payable	0	0
Pre-tax profit	100	100
Taxation @ 20%	-20	-20
Post tax profit	80	80
Shares in issue (million)	1000	900
EPS(p)	8	8.9
% change		11.11%
Share price(p)	160	80
PE ratio	20	
Earnings yield (EPS/Price)	5%	
Market value (£m)	1600	
No of shares bought	100	
Cost (£m)	160	

Company executives such as Bob like share buybacks because more often than not their bonuses are linked to increasing the EPS. Buybacks are also useful for offsetting any new shares that have been issued for bonuses and share options. Company stockbrokers also encourage them because they can charge commission on the transactions.

But lots of Bob's shareholders are not happy. It turns out that the shares were not worth 160p at the time of the buyback. They were overvalued at this price because of their low growth prospects. One year later they are trading at 80p each – equivalent to a PE ratio of 9 on the higher 8.9p EPS, and a fairer value for a company which isn't growing. The £160m spent on a share buyback at 160p has been a huge waste of money. The lesson here is that share buybacks only make shareholders better off if the price paid for the shares is less than the company is actually worth.

What Bob did was pay 160p per share for a business that was only really worth 80p per share. He was significantly overpaying for the shares and was wrongly focusing on the impact on EPS rather than the company's true value. In doing so, he reduced the true underlying value of the business to just over 71p (see Table 9.4). If he had paid 75p, for example, then he would have increased the value of the business.

When it comes to share buybacks, the effect on EPS is irrelevant to shareholders. By paying too much, Bob has destroyed a large chunk of shareholder value just as many company managements do in the real world. Instead, he should have paid the surplus cash out to shareholders as a special dividend. This would have meant that they would have pocketed the cash. With the share buyback at an overvalued price, they are actually worse off because the underlying value of their shareholding has fallen – the cash spent has been wasted.

Spending cash on buying back shares reduces the total value of the business (because it has less cash). Value per share goes up if the business value shrinks by less than the reduction in the number of shares. You can only do this by buying back shares for less than their long-term value – which has, inevitably, a judgement element.

Table 9.4: Buying back shares of Bob's Book Store at 160p and 75p

Bob's Book Store	Buying back at 160p	Buying back at 75p
True value per share (p)	80	80
Shares in issue (m)	1000	1000
Value of business (£m) = A	800	800
Buyback price (p)	160	75
Shares bought (m)	100	100

Bob's Book Store	Buying back at 160p	Buying back at 75p
Cost of buyback = B	160	75
Value of business after buyback C =(A–B)	640	725
Shares in issue (m)	900	900
New true value per share (p)	71.1	80.6

Remember that the purpose of this example was to show how EPS can be unreliable. To return to why you should not rely on EPS:

1. *EPS may not resemble true cash profits*: Quite often a company's true cash profits are significantly more or less than its EPS (more often less).

2. *EPS may be based on profits that are unsustainably high or temporarily low*: This means that the PE ratio could be misleadingly low or high. This is a particular problem for cyclical companies.

If you aren't going to use the PE ratio to value a company, because it relies on EPS, what should you do? I go on to answer this in the following chapters.

10

CALCULATING A COMPANY'S CASH PROFITS

WE HAVE ALREADY seen in an earlier chapter that a company's cash flow is a better measure of its financial performance than its profits. This means it is vital that you use cash flow to value the company as well.

Before you do that, you have to work out an estimate of a company's cash profits. That is the focus of Chapter 10.

Free cash flow may not be the best measure for valuing companies

You might be asking why we need to bother with working out a company's cash profits given that we have seen that it is very easy to calculate a company's free cash flow per share.

You just have to make sure that the free cash flow numbers you are looking at are a reliable indication of what the company can produce year in, year out. If they are not then you could fall into the trap of buying a company which you think is growing its free cash flow and becoming more valuable when it isn't.

Just as company management can manipulate profits, it can manipulate cash flows as well – especially in the short run. It can do things such as cutting back on investing in new assets (capex). One of the quickest ways for a company to boost its cash flow is to reduce the amount of working capital – the amount of cash needed for a company to conduct its day-to-day operations – tied up in the business. Reducing working capital boosts a company's operating cash flow – the amount of cash coming in from trading activities. However, this boost might not be permanent and might confuse an investor into thinking that a company's sustainable cash flow is higher than it might be in reality.

Annual cash flows can also be distorted by individual cash flows, such as tax refunds, pension fund top ups, litigation and restructuring costs. I'll show you how to deal with these in a short while.

Let's take a look at an example of a fictional situation in order to understand this better.

Close Cut Lawn Mowers plc

Close Cut is a maker of top quality lawn mowers. It has been consistently profitable but some of the big shareholders have become a bit frustrated with the company's cash flow performance. They reckon it's not as good as its competitors and can improve. If it does, there's a good chance the share price will go up.

The board of directors agrees and hires a hot shot new chief executive who comes with a big reputation for improving company cash flows. He sets up a simple plan to:

- Reduce the amount of finished products and spare parts held in stock. This has been running at 20% of annual sales. The new target is 15%.

- Get customers to pay their invoices quicker. Trade debtors (unpaid invoices at the year end) have been around 8% of sales. The target is to reduce this to 7%.

- Delay paying the company's suppliers and increase the amount of trade creditors. The target is to increase trade creditors from 15% to 17% of sales.

If the new boss is successful he will reduce the amount of working capital tied up in the business and improve operating and free cash flow. This project is his main priority before trying to grow sales and profits the following year.

Table 10.1 provides a summary of the company's profits, working capital position and free cash flow performance. The chief executive explains his grand plan to shareholders in the annual report.

The plan works. With profits staying the same as last year, cash flow improves dramatically. A reduction in stocks brings in £5m, faster paying customers brings in £1m and taking longer to pay suppliers brings in £2m.

Last year the change in working capital saw £2m of cash flow out of the company (the rows 'change in stocks', 'change in debtors' and 'change in creditors'). This year it has brought in £8m – a swing of £10m. Operating cash flow has improved from £28m to £38m and free cash flow has surged from £14m to £24m.

The previously grumpy shareholders are delighted. As the company has previously been valued at 10 times free cash flow, they reckon that this free cash flow improvement is going to increase its value from £140m to £240m and make them rich.

They are wrong. The improvements are not a permanent increase in cash flow.

Table 10.1: Close Cut Lawn Mowers' financial position

Close Cut Lawn Mowers plc	Last year	This year	Next year
Sales	100	100	105
Operating profit	20	20	21
Stocks	20	15	15.75
Trade debtors	8	7	7.35
Trade creditors	−15	−17	−17.85
Working capital	**13**	**5**	**5.25**
% sales			
Stocks	20%	15%	15%
Trade debtors	8%	7%	7%
Trade creditors	−15%	−17%	−17%
Working capital	13%	5%	5%
Operating cash flow			
Profit	20	20	21
Depreciation	10	10	10.5
Change in stocks	−2	5	−0.75
Change in debtors	−1	1	−0.35
Change in creditors	1	2	0.85
Operating cash flow	**28**	**38**	**31.25**
Tax paid	−4	−4	−4.2
Capex	−10	−10	−10.5
Free cash flow	**14**	**24**	**16.6**

Note: because these numbers are rounded they do not exactly add up.

Reality bites

Whilst the chief executive is celebrating his big bonus payment as a result of his efforts, he quickly sobers up when his finance director brings him down to earth with some harsh realities.

The amount of stock has been reduced to its limit. The warehouses are struggling to supply customers and provide spare parts. There's no way that stock levels can go lower than 15% of sales without compromising customer service.

Customers are complaining that they can't pay any faster without putting themselves in financial difficulties. The only way they will do so is if they can buy lawnmowers for 20% cheaper than they are now.

Suppliers are getting grumpy and don't want to be kept waiting any longer for their money. They feel they've been squeezed enough.

The chief executive's heart sinks. He knows that he has maxed out on the gains from squeezing working capital. He also knows that if there is no cash boost next year from changes in working capital, then operating and free cash flow will fall. This is exactly what happens, as you can see in the table.

Even with sales and profits growing, the ratio of working capital to sales stays the same and there is no significant cash flow improvement from it. You can see that if stocks, trade debtors and trade creditors all increase by the same 5% increase in sales there is a cash flow change from this working capital change of minus £0.25m. With no increase in cash flow from working capital as seen last year, free cash flow falls back to almost the same level as it was before.

The lesson here is to be wary of companies that boost their cash flow from decreases in working capital. Whilst such moves are welcome, they rarely lead to permanent improvements in free cash flow. You therefore need to be careful when valuing companies on the basis of free cash flow where such changes have occurred.

Fortunately, there is a way around this problem, which is to estimate a company's cash profits.

How to calculate a company's cash profits

Warren Buffett has looked at the cash profits of businesses for many years. In his 1986 letter to shareholders, he described how he worked out what he called the "owner earnings" (which I refer to as cash profits) of a business. He did this because he believed the reported profits of a business were not a conservative estimate of the amount of money that really belonged to the shareholders of a business.

Owner earnings are calculated as follows:

net income + depreciation & amortisation + other non cash items – maintenance capital expenditure

Buffett's view was that the amount of money a company needed to spend to maintain its competitive position (known as maintenance, or stay in business, capex) often exceeded the depreciation and amortisation expense, and therefore profits were overstated.

Also, if a business needed extra working capital (more stocks or more generous credit terms to customers), this should be added to the maintenance capex figure. Generally speaking, though, this calculation ignores changes in working capital that are included in free cash flow.

The hardest part of this calculation is trying to estimate what maintenance or stay in business capex is. As a company outsider without intimate knowledge of its assets and their condition it is virtually impossible for you to be exactly right on this.

But the good thing is, you don't need to be. The whole purpose is to get a figure for the amount of cash needed to keep fixed assets in good working order so that you can then have a conservative estimate of cash profits to value a company. Basing your valuation on a conservative figure is more prudent and lowers your chances of paying too much for a share, which in turn lowers your investment risk.

So how do you get an estimate of stay in business capex?

In my experience, there are three reasonable methods:

1. *The company tells you.* Some companies are very good at simply stating what the figure is. For example, Whitbread, the owner of Costa Coffee shops and Premier Inn hotels, gives this figure in its annual reports.

2. *Use a multiple of the current depreciation or amortisation expense.* In other words, use a figure that is bigger than this, such as 120%. This can be a reasonable estimate sometimes, but for some companies it can be way off if the cost of replacing assets is falling.

3. *Use a five- or ten-year average of capital expenditure or capex.* This is likely to include money spent to grow a business but these assets will need to be replaced in the future and so this could provide a good proxy for cash needed to stay in business. This is the approach I tend to use if the company does not state the figure outright.

Referring to Table 10.2, you can see that in some cases the annual depreciation expense is a lot less than the average five- or ten-year capex. This is the case in asset-intensive companies such as Anglo American (mining) and Tesco (supermarkets).

When you see this, it should not be surprising that both these companies have very poor free cash flow track records and modest ROCE and CROCI performances: two good reasons against investing in them. When I come across companies like this, I tend to avoid them unless they have been able to produce a good ROCE whilst investing heavily.

Media companies such as ITV, Sky and RELX often have capex which has been significantly less than depreciation and amortisation. Normally this kind of behaviour would make me suspicious. It might make me think that a company has been under-investing, which could hurt its ability to make more money in the future.

ITV has to spread the cost of things such as licences, customer contracts, software and programme libraries over their useful lives, which don't need to be matched by outflows of cash every year. I don't think there is anything bad going on here, but you need to study the company's history on this issue to make sure that it is not under-investing.

Table 10.2: Average capex spending compared with depreciation and amortisation

Company	Depreciation & amortisation (£m)	Capex 5y avg (£m)	Capex 10y avg (£m)
Anglo American	1664	3631	3082
Associated British Foods	482	699	625
BAE Systems	351	358	408
British American Tobacco	404	687	608
BT Group	2630	2500	2735
Capita	260	142	110
Domino's Pizza UK & IRL	7	7	9
ITV	94	59	54
Marks & Spencer Group	563	688	672
Next	113	114	125
RELX	520	314	261
Sky	762	523	435
Tesco	1332	2586	3083

Let's see how using average capex figures feeds through to an estimate of cash profits. As a rough rule of thumb, if the five-year capex figure is higher than the ten-year average you should use the higher figure.

As a recap, here's what you need to do:

- Take a company's most recent annual underlying or normalised net income/profit.

- Add back depreciation and amortisation.

- Take away an estimate of stay in business capex

- Divide by the weighted average number of shares in issue for the latest financial year to get an estimate of cash profit per share.

Table 10.3 shows the results of this process for three of the companies from Table 10.2.

Table 10.3: Estimating a company's cash profits

Cash profits (£m)	Domino's Pizza	ITV	Tesco
Net income	60.1	591.0	468.2
Deprec. & Amort.	6.6	94.0	1332.0
Stay in business capex	-8.9	-58.6	-3083.4
Cash profit	57.8	626.4	-1283.2
as % of net income	96.2%	106.0%	-274.1%
Shares (million)	498.2	4002.0	8126.0
Cash profit per share (p)	11.60	15.65	-15.79

As you can see, the key outlier here is Tesco. If you come across a company that looks as if it is losing money when estimating its cash profits you need to either do some more research to see if you have missed something – such as the company investing in lots of new assets rather than replacing them – or look for another share to buy.

Now that we have a company's cash profits, we can move on to look at how to use these to value shares.

11

USING CASH PROFITS TO VALUE SHARES

LET'S STAY WITH Domino's Pizza and use it as an example to show how to value it using its cash profits. I describe three different types of share valuation approaches:

1. *A cash yield or interest rate.* Once you have this, you can compare it with the interest rates on savings accounts or bonds.

2. *Earnings power value (EPV)*: This is the value of the shares if the current cash profits continue forever. This allows you to work out how much of the current share price can be explained by current cash profits and how much is explained by future growth in profits. The stronger the relationship to current profits, the cheaper the share is likely to be.

3. *A maximum target share price*: Setting a maximum share price for the shares based on the yield on government bonds and using that to set your target buying price.

Let's now work through each of these methods in turn.

1. Cash yield or interest rate

This approach is very simple. You take the cash profit per share and divide it by the current share price to get a cash interest rate (or yield).

cash interest rate = cash profit per share/share price

So for Domino's at 320p per share and with a cash profit per share of 11.6p (see Table 10.3), the cash interest rate is:

11.6p/320p = 3.62%

What does this mean?

3.62% is a pretty low interest rate. It may be higher than what you can get on savings accounts or bonds, but you have to ask yourself if it is high enough for you to take on the risk of owning the shares and the possibility of losing money.

The whole point of owning shares is to get a higher return on your money so that you can grow the value of your savings. If you are going to get only a small cash interest rate on your shares at the current share price, it could be a sign that the shares are overvalued. What a low interest rate is telling you is that cash profits are going to have to grow a lot in the future to allow you to get a decent return from owning the shares. If you look at Table 11.1, you will see why I have said this.

As I have said earlier in this book, investing is all about interest rates. To make money you should aim to try and get the highest rate of interest on your investments as you can without taking lots of unnecessary risks.

Only you can decide what rate of interest is high enough. Let's say that you want to get a 10% cash flow return on buying shares in Domino's at 320p. You would currently be getting 3.6%. You need to work out what annual rate of growth over what length of time would be needed to get to 10%.

The best way to do this is set up a spreadsheet and play around with some growth scenarios. In Table 11.1, I've assumed 10% annual cash profit growth. I then divide the cash profits by the current/buying price to get a cash yield on that price.

So, for example, in year 3 the cash profit per share is 15.4p, having grown at 10% per year over the previous three years. Dividing the share price of 320p by 15.4p and multiplying by 100 gives a cash yield of 4.8%.

As you can see, with 10% annual growth for ten years, you still don't quite get a 10% cash return on a buying price of 320p.

This kind of exercise can teach you a great deal about what a 320p share price for Domino's says for the company's future cash profits. As we saw with our DCF valuation in Chapter 9, a lot of future growth is already baked into the share price. By this, I mean that it takes a reasonably long time with a reasonably high growth rate to get a reasonable cash yield on buying the shares at 320p.

Profits are going to have to grow faster than 10% per year to get to an acceptable cash yield in a shorter time. Even if you wanted a 7% return, you would have to wait seven years at a 10% growth rate. That's a long time to wait.

And then what if growth is a lot lower than 10%, or even if profits fall? The chances are that Domino's share price would fall, which means you could end up losing money.

Table 11.1: Domino's Pizza growth and cash yields on buying price

Year	Cash profit (p)	Change (%)	Buying price (p)	Cash yield (%)
0	11.6		320	3.6
1	12.8	10	320	4.0
2	14.0	10	320	4.4
3	15.4	10	320	4.8
4	17.0	10	320	5.3
5	18.7	10	320	5.8
6	20.6	10	320	6.4
7	22.6	10	320	7.1
8	24.9	10	320	7.8
9	27.4	10	320	8.6
10	30.1	10	320	9.4

The low cash yield means that you are paying for growth in advance of it happening. It will take years of high growth in cash profits to get a reasonable return on your 320p buying price. This is one of the most risky things that you can face as an investor. You can protect yourself by insisting on a higher starting interest rate when buying shares in the first place. Personally, I would look for an interest rate of at least 5%, and even then I would have to be very confident that growth would be high for many years in the future.

To set your buying price for a 5% initial cash yield you take the cash profit per share and divide it by 5% or 0.05. For Domino's with a cash yield of 11.6p, this gives:

11.6p/0.05 = 232p

If you were even more cautious and wanted a starting yield of 8%, then your buying price would be:

11.6p/0.08 = 145p

These results of 232p and 145p make Domino's shares look well overpriced at 320p.

I'll have a bit more to say about this approach later in this chapter.

2. Earnings power value (EPV)

Another way to weigh up the value of a share is to calculate something known as its earnings power value (EPV). This gives you an estimated value of a share if its current cash profits stay the same forever. Here's how you calculate it:

1. Take a company's normalised or underlying trading profits or EBIT.

2. Add back depreciation and amortisation.

3. Take away stay in business capex.

4. Tax this cash profit number by the company's tax rate. If this is below the statutory corporation tax rate for the UK then consider using that rate (19% for 2017–18) in order to be conservative with your valuation.

5. Divide by a required interest rate to get an estimate of total company or enterprise value. There is plenty of academic research on what interest rate you should use when valuing a business. Most of it has been shown to be deeply flawed. All you need to know is that the higher the interest rate you use, the more conservative your estimate of value will be. I have used 8% for Domino's. Here are some rough and ready guidelines of the interest rates you might want to use when valuing different companies:

   - Large and less risky companies (FTSE 350): 7% to 9%.

   - Smaller and more risky (lots of debt or volatile profits): 10% to 12%.

   - Very small and very risky: 15% or more.

6. Take away debt, pension fund deficit, preferred equity and minority interests to get a value of equity. Add any surplus cash.

7. Divide by the number of shares in issue to get an estimate of EPV per share.

You should always use the number of shares that are in issue at the time of your valuation rather than the number shown in the last annual report. At the end of 2015. Domino's had 166.8 million fully paid up shares in issue according to note 30 of its accounts.

However, the number of shares in issue tends to change throughout the year. New shares can be issued to satisfy employee bonus awards whilst a company may have a policy of buying back its own shares. Companies can also change the number of shares in issue for a variety of other reasons. This means that the number of shares in issue can be quite different from the number shown in the last annual report. In June 2016, Domino's implemented a share split and subdivision of its share capital. This has the effect of reducing its shares in issue to just under 498 million. When I was valuing the company in late summer 2016 the company had 498.2m shares in issue. Obtaining the right number of shares for your valuation is fairly straightforward. The data is freely available on the internet from websites such as Google Finance or Yahoo Finance.

Table 11.2. shows how this calculation works for Domino's based on its 2015 accounts.

Table 11.2: Domino's Pizza earnings power value (£m), 2015

Underlying EBIT	73.6
Depreciation & Amortisation	6.6
Stay in business capex	-8.9
Cash trading profit	71.3
Tax @ 20%	-14.3
After tax cash profits (A)	**57.0**
Interest rate (B)	**8%**
EPV = A/B	**713**
Adjustments	
Net debt/net cash	40.4
Preference Equity	0
Minority interests	0
Pension fund deficit	0
Equity value	**753.4**
Shares in issue (m)	498.2
EPV per share (p)	**151.2**
Current share price (p)	320
EPV as % of current share price	47.3%
Future growth as % of current share price	52.7%

Compare your estimate of EPV per share with the current share price. With Domino's, we can see that the estimate of EPV accounts for less than half of the existing share price. A large chunk of the current 320p price is based on the expectation of future profit growth. This is a similar conclusion to our cash yield valuation earlier in this chapter.

EPV can be a great way of spotting very cheap shares. Sometimes it is possible to find shares which are selling at a significant discount to their EPV. When you come across a share like this, you need to spend time considering whether its current profits can stay the same, grow, or whether they are likely to fall. If profits are likely to fall, it might be best to move on and start looking at other shares.

To minimise the risk of overpaying for a company's shares, you should try to buy when its current profits – its EPV – can explain as much of the current share price as possible. As a rough rule of thumb, even if profits and cash flows have been growing rapidly, do not buy a share where more than half its share price is reliant on future profits growth. This would mean *not* buying Domino's at 320p per share in this example.

3. Setting a maximum price

What is the right price to pay for a quality company?

There is no right answer to this question, but it is something that every investor should think about. The first thing to acknowledge is that you are unlikely to find high-quality companies at bargain basement prices, except perhaps after a stock market crash. You are going to have to pay up in most cases. But how much is too much?

The trouble is that low interest rates on savings accounts and government bonds in recent years have pushed up the price of shares in general, and the shares of many high-quality blue chips, such as branded consumer goods companies, in particular. These companies' profits are seen to be highly reliable, as they come from regular purchases, and are regarded as being similar to cash flows from bonds. This means that the shares of companies such as Unilever, Reckitt Benckiser, Coca-Cola and Diageo have come to be known as 'bond proxies'.

Warren Buffett has a very simple approach to the valuation of companies with steady, predictable and growing cash flows. He calculates a company's owner earnings or cash profits (just as we have done above), and divides this by the current yield to maturity (gross redemption yield) on government bonds. So if he calculates a company has cash profits of 10p per share and bond yields are 5%, the maximum value of the share is 200p (10p/5%, or 10/0.05).

Another way of looking at this 200p maximum valuation is that it is equivalent to a PE multiple, or price to free cash flow, of 20 times. This can be found by dividing 1 by the bond yield (or your target yield from a share investment) of 5% (1/5% = 20).

You will note that if we multiply the cash profits per share of 10p by the PE multiple of 20, this gives the same maximum valuation for the shares of 200p.

The problem with this approach at the time of writing in 2016 is that bond yields have been pushed lower and lower in recent years and are close to zero – and even negative – in some countries. The ten-year UK government bond yield – an interest rate commonly used to value shares – in July 2016 was just 0.9%.

Figure 11.1 shows the yield on ten-year UK government bonds (gilts) compared with the rate of inflation since 1984. As you can see, there has often been a big gap between gilt yields and inflation, which means there was an after-inflation, real return on gilts. Since 2008, this gap has become smaller and has even turned negative (bond yields have been less than the rate of inflation) for some periods. This is reinforced by Figure 11.2, which charts the gap between gilt yields and inflation.

If you were to follow the Buffett approach to valuing shares and use this interest rate to value shares – by dividing their cash profits by 0.9% – then it would be telling you that shares were very cheap. For example, it would be saying that with Domino's delivering a cash yield of 11.6p, the maximum value of Domino's shares is 11.6p/0.9% (or 11.6p/0.009), which equals 1289p!

Figure 11.1: UK ten-year gilt yields and RPI inflation (%)

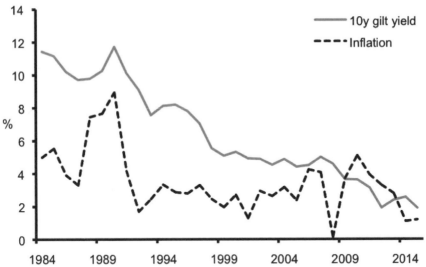

Figure 11.2: Gap between gilt yields and inflation (%)

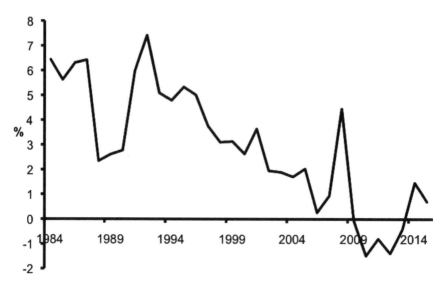

Looking at this from the direction of the PE multiple, it would be saying that to achieve your target interest rate of 0.9% you need to be looking for shares with a multiple of 111 (1/0.9% = 111). Once again, that puts the Domino's maximum valuation at 1289p (111 x 11.6p).

This is clearly unrealistic and the effect will be the same with other shares that you come to value as well. This means you need to make some kind of adjustment for these low interest rates on bonds so that you don't end up paying silly prices for quality companies.

You could look at the average gilt yield over the last 30 years – which is around 6.4% – and set a price limit on cash earnings at that yield, which equates to a cash profit multiple of 15.6 times (1 divided by 6.4%).

The thing is, you might not find many high-quality shares to buy at this price limit. And indeed, if you can't find any quality companies' shares at a decent price this might be telling you not to invest, which could be the right thing to do. Don't compromise on quality just to find something cheaper. You might live to regret it.

Another alternative is to add something extra to the current gilt yield instead to try and protect yourself from paying too much. Over the last 30 years, the average gap between gilt yields and inflation has been 2.93%. We can round this up to 3% and say that gilt yields have averaged 3% more than inflation.

So, if we take the rate of UK inflation in July 2016 of 1.4% and add 3% to it this, it would give a minimum cash yield of 4.4%, or a maximum cash profit multiple of 22.7 times (1 divided by 4.4%).

These may look like very rich valuations to many investors compared with days gone by and they are. However, if interest rates stay low – and possibly go lower – then it is a possibility that many shares of quality companies could have these kind of valuations attached to them. If that is the case, you should not buy the shares but wait for them to become cheaper.

One caveat here is that to command high valuations, companies need to be able to keep on growing their profits and cash flows over the coming years (ten years at least). If they don't then you will have paid too high a price and you stand a good chance of losing money.

Let's now look at an example of setting a target price for Domino's.

Setting a price target for Domino's Pizza shares

Let's put this theory into practice and set a maximum price and an ideal price to buy Domino's Pizza shares. Table 11.3 shows you how to calculate this.

This approach is saying that Domino's shares are currently too expensive to buy. The most you should pay is 263p per share, compared with a current share price of 320p. If you want even more of a buffer compared with the maximum price – a good rule of thumb is 15% – you will only want to pay 224p.

Table 11.3: Setting a maximum price and buying price for Domino's Pizza shares

Current cash profit per share (p) [see Table 10.3]	11.6
Divide by interest rate [UK inflation + 3%]	4.4%
Maximum price (p) (cash profit/interest rate)	**263.6**
Current price (p)	320
Ideal price at 15% discount (p)	**224**
Cash yield at ideal price (cash profit/ideal price)	5.18%

You might be waiting a long time for a share to reach your target price and it might never do so. However, it is far better to wait or even risk missing out on the few shares that are too expensive than to risk paying too much and lose money.

This kind of analysis can also give you some guidance of when to sell a share. If a share that you own reaches a maximum price it doesn't mean that you should automatically sell it. Shares can and do go beyond and below their fair valuations. In the case of Domino's above, I would not sell at 263p but if the share price exceeded this by 25% (329p), I might sell and then look for something cheaper to buy.

The importance of growth

I'd like to finish the chapter about valuation with a few notes about the importance of growth and how high share prices can unravel very quickly when profits stop growing.

Companies which investors like tend to command very high valuations because they are growing turnover and profits rapidly, or are expected to do so. By this I mean that their shares will have very high multiples of profits and cash flows, and very low yields attached to them.

This can persist for a long time but the dangers for investors of owning expensive or highly-rated shares can be significant when profits stop growing. This was the case with Restaurant Group in early 2016.

The company had been growing its profits at a healthy rate and was expected to continue doing so. The shares, priced at over 700p, were trading at over 20 times earnings. It then released a series of profit warnings which ended up with expectations for falling rather than rising profits. The valuation halved to just over 10 times earnings as the share price dropped. This is illustrated in Figure 11.3.

Investors in the shares lost nearly 60% of their investment and learned a brutal lesson of the high risks of owning expensive or highly-rated shares. This experience has been repeated countless times in the past and will surely happen many times again in the future.

The bottom line here is that if you are going to buy and own expensive shares, you must be very confident that high rates of growth can continue for a long time into the future. Because humans tend to be bad predictors of the future you need to protect yourself by not paying too high a price for shares.

This chapter has shown you how to value shares and to explain the crucial relationship between cash profits and interest rates.

I have shown a powerful way of working out how much of a company's current share price is based on its current profits and how much is related to future profits growth. I have also shown the importance of profits growth in valuing shares and how to work out how to not pay too much.

Figure 11.3: Restaurant Group share price, July 2015 to July 2016

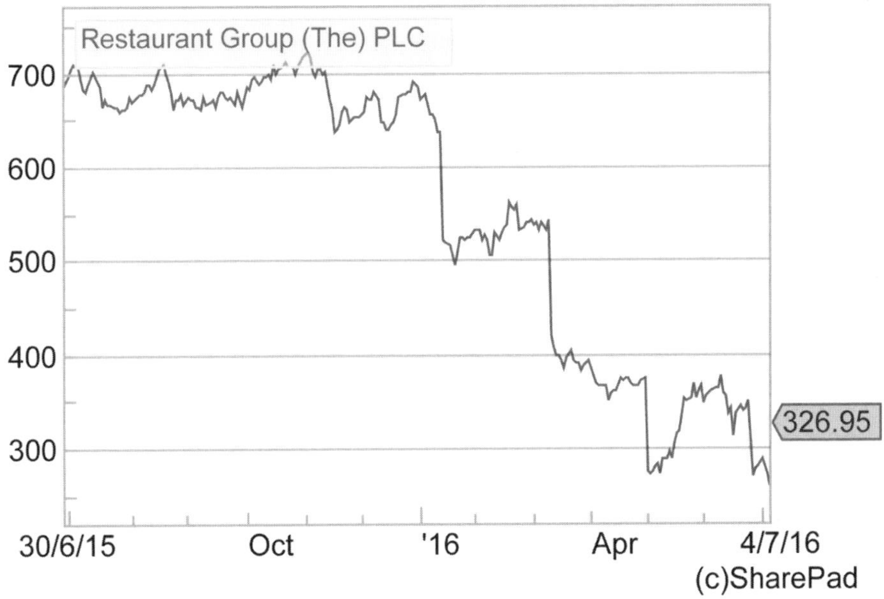

Final thoughts on valuation – can quality be more important than price?

Paying too much for a share can result in disappointing returns. No company, no matter how good, is a buy at any price. In this chapter, I have given you the tools to work out how much to pay for the shares of quality companies. Bear in mind that share valuation is not an exact science. Your valuation will never be exactly right, but by setting yourself some limits, you can reduce the risks that come from overpaying for shares.

However, there is some evidence to suggest that paying what might seem to be a moderately expensive price (slightly more than the suggested maximum) for a quality business can still pay off in the long run. The caveat here is that you have to be prepared to own shares for a very long time. Perhaps forever.

The way people invest is changing. Many people are not building a portfolio of shares during their working lives to cash in when they retire. An increasing number will have a portfolio that may remain invested for the rest of their lives. For them a portfolio of high-quality shares of durable companies may help provide them with a comfortable standard of living, with the initial price paid for the shares not being too big a consideration.

And despite trying to put a precise value on a share, we have to remember that the shares of high-quality businesses are scarce. This scarcity has a value and might mean that investors undervalue the long-term value of them.

The ability of high-quality companies to earn high returns on capital for a long time can create fabulous wealth for their shareholders. This is essentially how investors such as Warren Buffett have built their fortune.

In the Appendices, I show some examples of high-quality companies with high and stable returns on capital that have created substantial wealth over the decade from 2007 to 2016. Few if any of the shares could have been bought for really cheap prices. In many of the cases, the enduring quality and continued growth of the company could be seen to have been more important than the initial price paid for them.

PART 3 SUMMARY

HOW TO VALUE SHARES

IF YOU ARE to be a successful investor in shares, you need to pay particular attention to the price you pay for them. The biggest risk you face is paying too much. It is important to remember that no matter how good a company is, its shares are not a buy at any price.

Paying the right price is just as important as finding a high-quality and safe company. Overpaying for a share makes your investment less safe and exposes you to the risk of losing money.

Be careful not to be too mean with the price you are prepared to pay for a share. Obviously you want to buy a share as cheaply as possible, but bear in mind that you usually have to pay up for quality. Waiting to buy quality shares for very cheap prices may mean that you end up missing out on some very good investments. Some shares can take years to become cheap and many never do.

When valuing shares, you can use the following checklist to remind you of the process to follow:

1. You should value companies using an estimate of their cash profits.

2. Work out the cash yield a company is offering at the current share price. Is it high enough?

3. Calculate a company's earnings power value (EPV) to work out how much of a company's share price is explained by its current profits and how much is dependent on future profits growth. Do not buy shares where more than half the current share price is dependent on future profits growth.

4. Work out the maximum price you will pay for a share. Try and buy shares for less than this value. I suggest a discount of at least 15%.

5. The interest rate you use to calculate the maximum price should be at least 3% more than the rate of inflation.

6. You must be very confident in continued future profits growth to pay a price at or beyond the valuations in this book.

7. The higher the price you pay for profits/turnover/growth, the more risk you are taking with your investment. If profits stop growing, then paying an expensive price for a share can lead to substantial losses.

Appendices

APPENDIX 1

THE POWER OF LEASE-ADJUSTED ROCE

I HAVE ARGUED IN this book that calculating a lease-adjusted ROCE is a better way to measure a company's financial performance than using the standard ROCE figure.

But does it add up to better investment results?

One of the simplest and most effective investing strategies is something known as Magic Formula investing. It was devised by US investor Joel Greenblatt and is described in his excellent book, *The Little Book That Beats The Market*.

Greenblatt's strategy is based on two criteria:

1. *Buying high-quality companies*: ones with a high return on capital employed (ROCE).

2. *Buying cheap companies*: ones with a high earnings yield. Where earnings yield is defined as EBIT divided by a company's enterprise value (EV). EV is a company's market capitalisation plus its net borrowings (total borrowings less cash).

Greenblatt's book sets out an impressive market-beating track record. From 1988 to 2009, a Magic Formula portfolio delivered average annual returns of 23.8% per year, compared with 9.6% for the S&P 500 index. It had some stellar years, with returns of over 70% in 1991 and 2001, and over 80% in 2003.

However, it had a bad year in 2008, losing nearly 40%. This was worse than the S&P 500. In recent years, it has not done as well, with Greenblatt suggesting that the formula does not fare well when stock markets are rising strongly.

The Magic Formula strategy has similarities with what I have set out in this book – namely buying good companies at good prices. However, Greenblatt's approach ignores the value of hidden debts when calculating ROCE and EV: he does not suggest looking at the lease-adjusted ROCE and lease-adjusted earnings yield.

For the year 2016, I set up two Magic Formula portfolios. I ranked the shares in the FTSE All-Share index on the basis of combined score for their ROCE and EBIT yield. A 20-share portfolio was selected based on the highest combined rankings. The 20 shares selected were from 20 different sectors of the stock market, to create a diversified portfolio. One 20-share portfolio was based on the original Greenblatt formula, whereas the other was based on lease-adjusted ROCE and lease-adjusted EBIT yield. The two portfolios were opened at the start of 2016 and closed at the end of the year.

The results are shown in Table A1. Also shown in the table are the results of buying the top 20 shares ranked by lease-adjusted EBIT yield alone. This is a way to buy shares based on cheapness alone.

Table A1: The results of a 2016 Magic Formula portfolio test

Portfolio	Starting value	Closing value	Total return	Gainers	Losers
Simple Magic Formula	£100,000	£121,749	21.75%	14	6
Lease-adjusted Magic Formula	£100,000	£143,575	43.58%	13	7
Lease-adjusted EBIT yield	£100,000	£140,193	40.19%	12	8

Both portfolios beat the 16.8% total return (share price change + dividends received) of the FTSE All-Share index. However, the lease-adjusted portfolio trounced the simple magic formula and produced double the returns. As you can see, the lease-adjusted Magic Formula outperformed the straight cheap portfolio (lease-adjusted EBIT yield) too.

Whilst one year's results are by no means conclusive that lease-adjusted ROCE investing is better, 2016 does indicate the power of this approach compared to the standard calculation of ROCE.

That said, I do not believe that successful investing boils down to just two numbers. By applying the analysis techniques in this book I think it is possible to buy shares in good, safe companies at a price that will reward the patient and long-term investor.

APPENDIX 2

FTSE 100 DATA

TABLE A2 SHOWS data for 76 companies from the FTSE 100 index as at January 2017. Banks and insurance companies are not included in the table, as they do not suit this type of analysis.

The table includes the following ten-year averages:

1. ROCE;

2. lease-adjusted ROCE;

3. lease-adjusted CROCI;

4. capex to operational cash flow;

5. free cash flow dividend cover.

The companies in the table are ranked by ten-year average lease-adjusted ROCE, because this is a good place to start when analysing companies as investments.

The purpose of this table is to illustrate the kinds of results being generated for these measures by FTSE 100 companies. If you refer to Part 1 (and for quick reference the summary at the end of Part 1), you can see the results for these measures that I demand in companies I am going to invest in.

Table A2: FTSE 100 constituent results for measures of investment quality

TIDM	Name	ROCE 10y avg	Lease-adj ROCE 10y avg (7x, 7%)	Lease-adj CROCI 10y avg (7x, 7%)	Capex to op. cash flow 10y avg	FCF div cover 10y avg
HL.	Hargreaves Lansdown	108.3	97.9	62.9	4.0	1.5
MCRO	Micro Focus International	44.8	36.6	30.3	13.1	2.3
PPB	Paddy Power Betfair	47.0	32.9	34.9	21.9	1.5
SKY	Sky	31.8	29.7	22.8	31.3	1.8
NXT	Next	55.8	29.3	21.5	18.5	2.6
FRES	Fresnillo	27.9	27.3	10.7	56.8	−3.7
RB.	Reckitt Benckiser Group	25.0	24.3	19.0	9.3	2.0
BLT	BHP Billiton	26.0	24.2	11.0	50.5	1.8
AZN	AstraZeneca	24.9	24.2	17.0	25.9	1.7
BATS	British American Tobacco	24.3	23.6	14.9	13.4	1.0
GSK	GlaxoSmithKline	24.3	23.6	14.3	23.9	1.0
IHG	InterContinental Hotels Group	23.0	22.0	17.7	24.5	2.2
CRDA	Croda International	22.6	21.9	9.9	-0.4	0.9
ANTO	Antofagasta	20.7	20.6	12.2	54.2	0.4
ITRK	Intertek Group	24.3	19.2	13.6	29.7	2.2
SN.	Smith & Nephew	20.1	19.0	10.4	31.9	2.4
ULVR	Unilever	20.3	18.9	11.9	25.3	1.3
BRBY	Burberry Group	30.2	18.8	12.5	29.9	2.0
SGE	Sage Group (The)	19.8	18.5	16.1	7.7	2.3
LSE	London Stock Exchange Group	19.4	17.7	15.3	12.8	2.9
ITV	ITV	18.4	17.7	13.9	20.1	1.9
RDSB	Royal Dutch Shell	17.6	17.5	3.1	59.2	0.5
CNA	Centrica	17.3	17.3	7.6	47.8	0.9
RIO	Rio Tinto	17.2	16.9	6.8	50.2	2.3

TIDM	Name	ROCE 10y avg	Lease-adj ROCE 10y avg (7x, 7%)	Lease-adj CROCI 10y avg (7x, 7%)	Capex to op. cash flow 10y avg	FCF div cover 10y avg
DGE	Diageo	17.2	16.8	11.1	16.5	1.3
CPG	Compass Group	19.4	16.7	13.3	27.7	2.0
HIK	Hikma Pharmaceuticals	16.6	16.6	9.1	48.9	1.9
CPI	Capita	19.2	15.8	13.2	24.3	1.9
REL	RELX	16.0	15.1	17.4	14.9	2.4
JMAT	Johnson Matthey	15.2	15.0	6.9	51.5	1.3
SMIN	Smiths Group	15.5	14.9	18.0	20.1	2.7
EXPN	Experian	14.4	14.2	15.3	25.1	2.7
BNZL	Bunzl	16.4	14.2	12.0	6.9	2.4
MKS	Marks & Spencer Group	15.5	13.7	9.1	51.3	1.4
IMB	Imperial Brands	13.4	13.3	11.4	9.7	1.8
SHP	Shire	12.9	13.2	19.2	22.5	12.5
BT.A	BT Group	14.2	13.1	10.0	55.4	1.6
PFG	Provident Financial	12.4	12.1	2.3	13.3	-0.2
BAB	Babcock International Group	12.8	12.0	10.7	19.7	2.2
PSN	Persimmon	12.1	12.0	12.6	2.0	5.8
BA.	BAE Systems	12.4	11.9	7.1	41.4	1.3
RRS	Randgold Resources Ltd	11.8	11.8	−0.3	116.7	−1.5
WTB	Whitbread	13.1	11.6	7.8	64.5	2.2
AHT	Ashtead Group	12.1	11.6	3.6	73.1	-0.2
AAL	Anglo American	11.7	11.6	4.0	66.6	1.0
SSE	SSE	11.9	11.2	3.2	98.6	0.2
WOS	Wolseley	12.3	11.0	8.9	77.8	2.4
ABF	Associated British Foods	11.4	10.9	5.3	57.7	1.2
BP.	BP	11.1	10.6	3.9	66.9	0.5
DC.	Dixons Carphone	10.7	10.6	3.9	268.4	1.9
EZJ	easyJet	11.1	10.3	1.9	112.2	0.4

TIDM	Name	ROCE 10y avg	Lease-adj ROCE 10y avg (7x, 7%)	Lease-adj CROCI 10y avg (7x, 7%)	Capex to op. cash flow 10y avg	FCF div cover 10y avg
DCC	DCC	10.4	10.2	9.3	32.4	2.2
RR.	Rolls-Royce Group	10.4	10.2	5.1	56.0	1.5
TSCO	Tesco	10.5	10.1	3.3	79.1	−1.7
GKN	GKN	10.1	9.9	3.8	84.8	0.7
MRW	Morrison (Wm) Supermarkets	9.9	9.8	3.7	62.2	1.1
MNDI	Mondi	9.7	9.7	6.6	54.6	1.3
WPP	WPP Group	9.9	9.3	7.7	17.9	2.4
NG.	National Grid	8.9	8.9	3.7	67.5	0.5
KGF	Kingfisher	9.3	8.6	6.2	45.9	2.2
SKG	Smurfit Kappa Group	8.5	8.4	6.7	38.6	2.8
INF	Informa	8.4	8.3	9.5	15.0	2.5
SBRY	Sainsbury (J)	8.2	7.9	2.0	92.0	−0.4
CRH	CRH	7.6	7.6	7.0	33.1	2.1
BDEV	Barratt Developments	7.6	7.5	6.5	2.0	1.5
SVT	Severn Trent	7.3	7.3	2.9	65.9	0.1
VOD	Vodafone Group	7.1	7.2	4.7	58.7	0.9
UU.	United Utilities Group	6.9	6.9	2.5	71.1	0.2
HMSO	Hammerson	6.4	6.4	−2.6	161.4	−3.3
SDR	Schroders	6.2	6.1	7.5	6.1	4.0
PSON	Pearson	5.9	6.0	7.3	20.2	1.6
TW.	Taylor Wimpey	5.5	5.5	5.6	7.1	2.4
INTU	Intu Properties	5.5	5.5	0.9	43.9	−1.7
CCL	Carnival	5.4	5.4	2.0	79.3	1.1
BLND	British Land Co	4.5	4.5	−1.2	181.8	−1.4
LAND	Land Securities Group	4.0	4.0	−0.1	94.5	−1.0

APPENDIX 3

HIGH-QUALITY COMPANIES AND SHAREHOLDER RETURNS (2007–2016)

I N THE TEN-YEAR period from the beginning of 2007 until the end of 2016, the FTSE All-Share index generated a cumulative total return (change in share price plus dividends received) of 72%.

The following 15 companies produced consistent and high returns on capital (ROCE), and delivered impressive total returns to their shareholders, in this period. I have provided a chart for each company to illustrate its lease-adjusted ROCE for the ten years.

Whilst I am not a fan of using the PE ratio to value companies (as explained in Part 3), I use it here on the grounds of simplicity to give an approximate guide to how cheap or expensive the shares were at the start of 2007. Quality companies tend to turn a high proportion of their profits into cash, so the PE can be seen as a proxy for a cash profits multiple.

On 1 January 2007, the redemption yield on 10-year UK government bonds was 4.63%. If you were using the Buffett valuation approach described in Part 3 of the book, without making any adjustments for inflation then the maximum multiple of cash profits you would pay would have been 21.6 times (one divided by 4.63%).

Note: Shareholder returns have been rounded to the nearest 10%.

AG BARR

Company	PE 1 January 2007	Total shareholder return 2007–2016
AG Barr	17.3	210%

www.sharepad.co.uk   ©SharePad

British American Tobacco

Company	PE 1 January 2007	Total shareholder return 2007–2016
British American Tobacco	14.6	300%

www.sharepad.co.uk   ©SharePad

Cranswick

Company	PE 1 January 2007	Total shareholder return 2007–2016
Cranswick	18.3	190%

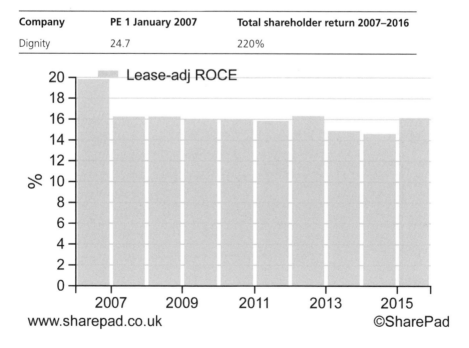

Dignity

Company	PE 1 January 2007	Total shareholder return 2007–2016
Dignity	24.7	220%

Diploma

Company	PE 1 January 2007	Total shareholder return 2007–2016
Diploma	14.2	570%

www.sharepad.co.uk ©SharePad

Domino's Pizza

Company	PE 1 January 2007	Total shareholder return 2007–2016
Domino's Pizza	30.9	550%

www.sharepad.co.uk ©SharePad

Fidessa

Company	PE 1 January 2007	Total shareholder return 2007–2016
Fidessa	35.4	180%

www.sharepad.co.uk   ©SharePad

InterContinental Hotels

Company	PE 1 January 2007	Total shareholder return 2007–2016
InterContinental Hotels	30.5	230%

www.sharepad.co.uk   ©SharePad

Paddy Power Betfair

Company	PE 1 January 2007	Total shareholder return 2007–2016
Paddy Power Betfair	19.1	870%

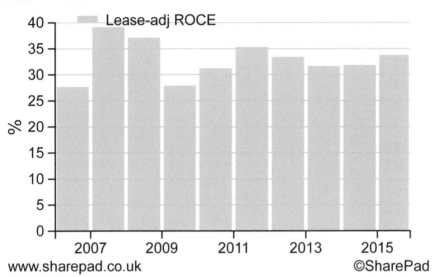

Reckitt Benckiser

Company	PE 1 January 2007	Total shareholder return 2007–2016
Reckitt Benckiser	21.9	240%

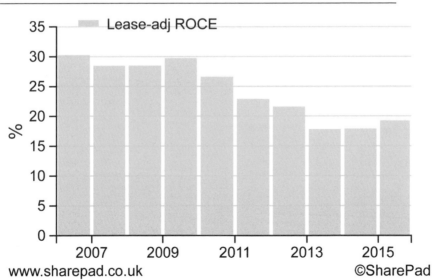

RELX

Company	PE 1 January 2007	Total shareholder return 2007–2016
RELX	16.0	200%

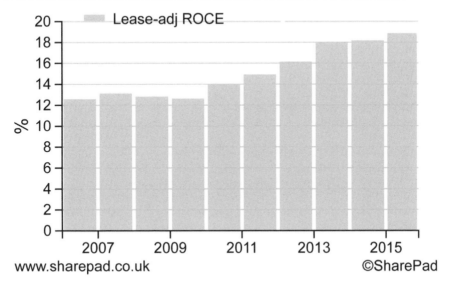

www.sharepad.co.uk   ©SharePad

Rightmove

Company	PE 1 January 2007	Total shareholder return 2007–2016
Rightmove	108.6	940%

www.sharepad.co.uk   ©SharePad

Sage

Company	PE 1 January 2007	Total shareholder return 2007–2016
Sage	21.9	170%

www.sharepad.co.uk ©SharePad

Spirax-Sarco

Company	PE 1 January 2007	Total shareholder return 2007–2016
Spirax-Sarco	17.5	380%

www.sharepad.co.uk ©SharePad

Unilever

Company	PE 1 January 2007	Total shareholder return 2007–2016
Unilever	17.6	180%

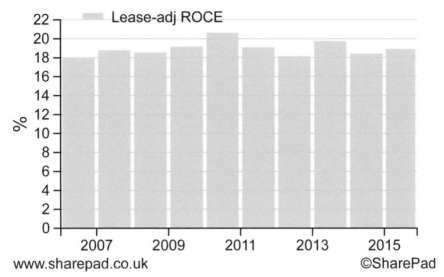

www.sharepad.co.uk · ©SharePad

APPENDIX 4

FTSE ALL-SHARE SECTOR ROCE ANALYSIS

Tᴀʙʟᴇ A4 sʜᴏᴡs data for sectors from the FTSE All-Share index as at January 2017. The following data is included:

1. average lease-adjusted ROCE

2. average lease-adjusted ROCE weighted by market capitalisation

3. the number of companies from each sector that have been included in the calculation of the average.

The purpose of this table is to illustrate which sectors of the stock market are more profitable than others. It is intended as a quick reference guide to show you where to look for quality shares and which sectors you might want to avoid.

There are two columns based on lease-adjusted ROCE. The first column is the standard version that has been used throughout this book. This is a ROCE calculation that is based on all the money (capital employed) invested by companies in their businesses. This is the version that I use when looking for quality shares.

Table A4: FTSE All-Share sector ROCE analysis (January 2017)

Sector	Average lease-adjusted ROCE	Weighted average lease-adjusted ROCE	Included
Aerospace & Defense	12.2	11.1	9 of 9
Automobiles & Parts	9.4	9.4	1 of 1
Beverages	13.1	12.1	5 of 5
Chemicals	16.8	18.4	7 of 7

Sector	Average lease-adjusted ROCE	Weighted average lease-adjusted ROCE	Included
Construction & Materials	9.7	6.8	15 of 15
Electricity	8.5	9.0	2 of 2
Electronic & Electrical Equipment	13.8	14.1	11 of 11
Equity Investment Instruments	0.3	0.7	173 of 175
Financial Services	12.8	14.1	32 of 32
Fixed Line Telecommunications	16.4	13.6	4 of 4
Food & Drug Retailers	9.4	7.3	7 of 7
Food Producers	10.6	12.6	8 of 8
Forestry & Paper	18.0	18.0	1 of 1
Gas, Water & Multiutilities	7.8	8.5	5 of 5
General Industrials	10.8	11.5	5 of 5
General Retailers	13.7	14.5	30 of 30
Health Care Equipment & Services	7.7	10.0	9 of 9
Household Goods & Home Construction	18.5	19.7	15 of 15
Industrial Engineering	12.6	14.2	12 of 12
Industrial Metals & Mining	6.9	6.5	2 of 2
Industrial Transportation	9.7	7.3	7 of 7
Leisure Goods	28.9	28.9	1 of 1
Media	65.3	49.1	21 of 21
Mining	6.5	6.7	18 of 18
Mobile Telecommunications	7.0	2.9	2 of 2
Oil & Gas Producers	0.8	1.2	9 of 9
Oil Equipment, Services & Distribution	6.2	3.2	7 of 7
Personal Goods	13	13.7	6 of 6
Pharmaceuticals & Biotechnology	6.9	12.0	12 of 12
Real Estate Investment & Services	9.0	10.8	20 of 20
Real Estate Investment Trusts	6.5	6.1	28 of 28
Software & Computer Services	22.6	18.4	12 of 12
Support Services	13.5	14.2	56 of 56
Technology Hardware & Equipment	−6.8	−2.1	5 of 5
Tobacco	15.1	17.4	2 of 2
Travel & Leisure	12.6	16.1	36 of 36

Source:SharePad

APPENDIX 5

GLOSSARY

Amortisation

An accounting expense used to match the cost of an intangible asset over its useful life. The annual amortisation expense reduces the balance sheet value of the intangible asset(s) concerned and is charged against a company's turnover – and therefore reduces profits.

Capex

The cash amounts spent on buying new fixed assets.

Current asset

An asset that is expected to be turned into cash within one year, such as stocks, debtors, cash and short-term investments.

Current operations

Parts of a company's business which it intends to own and trade from for the foreseeable future.

Depreciation

An accounting expense used to match the cost of a tangible asset over its useful life. The annual depreciation expense reduces the balance sheet value of the tangible asset(s) concerned and is charged against a company's turnover – and therefore reduces profits.

Earnings power value (EPV)

The value of a business if a set level of trading profits continue forever.

EBIT

Earnings before interest and tax. A company's trading or operating profit plus profits from joint ventures.

Fixed asset

An asset that is used in a business to generate revenues and profits, such as a building or plant or machinery.

Free cash flow (FCF)

The amount of cash left over after a company has paid all its non-discretionary costs. It is calculated by taking a company's operating cash flow less tax, interest paid, preference dividends and capex. It is the amount of cash that the company is free to pay to shareholders in a year.

Free cash flow to the firm (FCFF)

The amount of cash left over to pay lenders and shareholders. Operating cash flow less tax and capex.

Intangible fixed asset

Non-physical fixed assets, such as brands, patents, software licences or goodwill.

Joint venture

A business that is owned by two separate companies.

Non-current asset

An asset that is not expected to be turned into cash within one year. Mostly made up of a fixed asset.

Operating cash flow

The cash generated from a company's trading activities.

Operating leases

Expenses paid by a company to rent fixed assets.

Pension deficit

The excess of a final salary pension scheme's liability over the value of its assets.

Profit

Turnover less costs (expenses). There are many variants, e.g. EBIT, operating profit, pre-tax profit, post-tax profit.

Profit margin

The percentage of a company's sales that are turned into profits.

ROCE

A company's trading profit (EBIT) expressed as a percentage of the amount of money invested in the company (capital employed).

Share buyback

When a company uses its own money to buy its own shares from existing shareholders.

Tangible fixed asset

A physical fixed asset, such as a building or plant and machinery.

Working capital

The amount of money a company needs to carry on its day-to-day activities. It is a company's current assets less its current liabilities.

APPENDIX 6

WHERE TO FIND DATA

ALL THE DATA described is in each company's annual accounts, which are readily available online.

There are also numerous online and paper-based services for this sort of data, but the easiest single source is SharePad. In the spirit of full disclosure, I work for Ionic Information who created SharePad.

I played a significant role in designing SharePad and if you wish to put into practice the ideas in this book then SharePad can help you do that by giving you access to the data you need.

Nevertheless, the ideas in this book are worth understanding in their own right and they can be fully implemented by using a spreadsheet or other tools if you wish.

INDEX